Diary

of

a

Jailhouse

Lawyer

Tracy Green

The events and court cases in this book are not fictitious. The names in this book have been changed to protect the identities of the individuals and circumstances described.

BAM Publications

www.bampublications.com

Bampublications2015@gmail.com

ISBN: 153989780X

ISBN-13: 978-1539897804

Acknowledgements & Appreciations to…

BOMBA, From Miami Florida, Big "G" (George Morales), From Connecticut, Ivan Johnson From Harlem New York, Big Koola From Washington DC., Big Scoop, The young General from Yonkers, New York. As-Sadiq From Bergen County, New Jersey, Gotti Johnson and Tuquam, both from Brooklyn New York, Dakim, Born Allen, and Shakim Allah, From Bronx and Brooklyn New York. Sinbad Benzo ED, Mr. Tootie, Suge, Big Bones, One Punch, Tweet, Lil Dee, Keylow, Reese, Tray Kay, Chancey, and yes to you DOC HOLLADAY, all from California.

I love you all, and miss you all as well. So I dedicated this book- Volume One to you, my friends forever!

And to Ms. Morsey. Mr. Gage, Mr., Davis, Mr. Painter, Mr. Wagner, all of these gentle people who were the BEST counselors and Case Managers. Huck-B, King AGA, and Joka-Red. BOUT IT-BOUT IT, Mr. Kings, Ms. Atkins all the from Atlanta USP.

Mr. Holt and your brother Ray, Ronnie Holt, Mr. Scott Didrull, Wardens;

And yes to you Brooklyn Black, Michael Delancy, Hollywood, Ms. Sexton a beautiful lady, and you to Mr. Fed and Tolbert, From Buffalo New York.

No question to you Reverend Ortiz, from Coleman FCC. And how could I ever forget you Mr. Simmons, Duke, Ms. Torres, and Ms. Dennis and to you Mr. McCloud (City Court Judge)

And yes to you Mr. Pallidino from Buffalo New York. And to one of my best friends, Bo Joe (Joseph Elsten), Buffalo, New York.   Finally to you Nach, Neal Dobbins, Dee-Dee, Ikey Pain, Big-City Blue, and Joop. To a very good friend of mine, Slim Ratfield, the best guy I ever encountered.

If I never ever make it back to "FREEDOM," at least I died a Jail House Pro-Se Litigant, trying every single day with all my heart and soul, and all the intelligence within me...

This book is dedicated to "Nature Boy" AKA "Nach" and to Vivian Herrod AKA "Tookey" from Buffalo, New York.

Donald Green

Preface

This is a story that has its beginning near the Canadian border in a blue collar town generally known for its cold, snowy winters and the historic and majestic landmark such as Niagara Falls. It's Buffalo, New York, home of the National Football League's "Bills", the only NFL team to have lost three consecutive Super Bowls and the home of Donald "Sly" Green, a reputed drug Kingpin now convicted and languishing in a federal prison serving four life sentence terms of imprisonment and a one-hundred-and-ten-year sentence.

Raised in the poor black ghetto of this northern most city, Donald lived his young life with his mother and Grandmother. He was relatively a good kid growing up and obeyed his mother and Grandmother and minded his manners. As a very inquisitive kid, he would sit for hours on end reading books on all kinds of subjects- possessed with an insatiable desire to learn about new things.

From the very beginning, young Donald demonstrated an unusual fascination with the criminal underworld, in particular, "La Costra Nostra," commonly known as "THE MAFIA." He was intrigued by such charismatic figures as Alfonse Capone and Lucky Luciano- awed by the power they wield and the respect they commanded. It reminded him of the black gangsters of his own neighborhood and how they ruled their territories, just as the Italian mobsters ruled on their side of town.

The young lad began to discover what exactly these criminal organizations did- how they survived and ruled with fear and intimidation, maintaining a stranglehold on their interest, all amidst the local police and mostly with their approval.

Donald's many visits to the library were spent researching organized crime, viewing microfilm of old newspapers that chronicled gangster activities and anything that had a connection to the Mafia, all the way to the five families of New York City. Though young Donald had never broken the law up to this point of his youth, little did he know, his life of crime had already begun.

Several decades later, Donald Sly Green would find himself in the United States Penitentiary at Leavenworth, Kansas as a Federal Inmate- Number 39747-019- after having been wrongfully convicted on the fabricated testimony of career criminals for crimes committed under the super Kingpin ACT and RICO statutes. Now in the hot house and faced with a multitude of legal problems and the real possibility of never being a free man again, he walks into the prison law library and begins the arduous task of trying to win this freedom and so the diaries of a jailhouse lawyer begins...

CHAPTER ONE

ARREST, TRIAL, CONVICTION, AND SENTENCE

The New Year of 1992, did not ring in much promise or prosperity for me, Donald Sly Green. I had been arrested after a Federal grand jury, sitting for the Western District of New York, handed down a 73 count indictment charging me and numerous other co-defendants with violations of the Super Kingpin Act and RICO statutes. The charges included murder, drug trafficking, weapons possession, extortion, and many other criminal acts. The legal and media communities of Buffalo were all a buzz over the arrests and indictments. Patrons in the local restaurants and taverns were full of conversation and would anxiously await the evening's news broadcasts to hear of the latest developments regarding the arrest of Donald Sly Green and his co-defendants in this sensational case.

At the U.S. Attorney's office in the heart of the city, young, up and coming lawyers were frantically preparing the case against this notorious gangster, the likes of which Buffalo had not seen. Informants were cultivated and debriefed. Their testimonies scripted and rehearsed without regards for truthfulness as if these unprincipled characters were auditioning for a role in a new movie entitled "Lies and Deceit." Promises were made and unscrupulous deals were cut with these dishonest and shady criminals for reduced sentences and more. However, the Federal prosecutors assigned to the case were not so much concerned with the integrity of the evidence or the ethical standards they violate as they trudge roughshod over the Constitution of the United

8

States.

Nevertheless, I must prepare myself to defend the criminal charges against me with absolutely no knowledge of the law and how it worked. I must select a capable attorney whose decisions and strategies meet with my satisfaction. I choose Paul Cambria, a well-known and respected criminal trial attorney from Buffalo. Though I felt inadequate and totally out of my element, I trusted in the legal representation of this reputable barrister.

Trial begins amid a mass of security and media frenzy. The government's case rests entirely on the fabricated testimony of career criminals and rats, their only motives for taking the witness stand against me is to avoid the lengthy prison sentences they themselves are facing. Of course, with promises of money and a new life in the Federal witness protection, all expenses paid by the U.S. Department of Justice, they eagerly line up for a chance at this prize.

The vast legal resources of this Federal agency are unleashed on me and make no mistake about it, I was no match for its furor. And so begins the true tale of how I came face to face with the awesome power of the Office of the United States Attorney and how I proceed in defending myself against its unrelenting onslaught.

After an eight week trial I was convicted on multiple counts of the indictment. It was no surprise especially after observing firsthand how the government had so meticulously stacked the deck against me. However, it took many months for the ramification of the verdict to actually sink in.

Sentencing on the charges was put off until a presentence investigation report could be compiled by the U.S. Department of Probation. This document is generally referred to as the "PSI" and contains the factual background of a convicted defendant's family, education, employment, mental and physical health, and criminal histories. No stone is left unturned in the gathering and reporting of this information. It is a lengthy document and requires several months to complete. Any information not factually reported in the PSI can be challenged before the court at a hearing that is held for that purpose.

At the sentencing hearing and after judicial review of the PSI, I was sentenced to four life terms of imprisonment, plus one hundred and ten years, all to run consecutive to each other. To say this is a lifetime is an understatement.

Now committed to the Custody of the Attorney General, the U.S. Marshall's Service transported me under a heavily armed security detail, to the Federal Correctional Institution at Otisville, New York. After arrival at this medium security facility, I was placed in solitary confinement for security concerns because of my high profile status. I would remain at this Bureau of Prison's facility until the Designation and Sentencing Computation Center (DSCC) at Grand Prairie, Texas made the appropriate designation based on the correct scoring of my security level assignment.

It was here at FCI-Otisville that I initially began to explore the legal options available to me.

Counsel filed a Notice of Appeal in the Second Circuit Court of Appeals. Trying to make sense of all of the different motions and briefs being filed by my legal team and those of the government, comprehending the legalese, was a work in progress. Even so, I never became discouraged and plowed ahead, trying to learn everything I could. With the help of other fellow inmates who were more so versed in the law, I slowly began to find my way.

I learned how to select the proper book for whatever the subject was I might be researching. I could distinguish between the difference in the United States Code Annotated volumes and those of the United States Supreme Court Reports. The more I would read, the more I would learn. Nonetheless, any thoughts about becoming a jailhouse lawyer were the farthest thing from my mind.

CHAPTER TWO

LEAVENWORTH, KANSAS
UNITED STATES FEDERAL PENITENTIARY

It was early morning when the dingy gray walls of the limestone and steel monstrosity, known simply as USP-Leavenworth, came into view. The sun was not shining. It was misting rain. With my homie, Capone, a loyal soldier from the neighborhood, sitting right next to me, and thirty-eight others, the BOP's transport bus rolled ever closer. Capone was a very good friend from the hood. I was sure that we would be able to make this trip together into the unknown world that lay ahead behind those high walls topped by gun towers.

Capone was more fortunate in the sentence he received than myself. Capone accepted the government's plea agreement offer for a lesser sentence, as he was not the major player in the criminal enterprise. However, know this from the jump, Capone is no rat and never ever entertained becoming a puppet for the government. He's straight stand-up! Don't get it messed up!

Despite the fact that I was now entering a United States Penitentiary for the very first time, the front view kind of reminded me of the White House, instead of a "Dangerous Federal Penitentiary". I was somewhat in awe of the place and a little apprehensive about not really knowing what awaited me on the inside. Whatever it would be, I planned to meet it head on. Wasn't gonna be no fakin! And that's a true bill.

All of the inmates on the bus were blackboxed - a special security apparatus designed to place maximum restriction on hand-cuff manipulation and escape proof. It also would cut into your wrists and leave them red and swollen.   The bus had to enter a special sallyport area and checked before being passed thru to the inside. Once inside, it proceeded to the Receiving and Discharge (R&D). There we were called one at a time by name to come to the front of the bus and recite our register number. Placed in holding pens and unshackled, we were processed by being humiliated and ordered to strip naked. We were interviewed by staff, bombarded with questions, medical, security screening, etc. and then given a bag lunch to quench the hunger. After this three hour ordeal, myself and Capone were released to the population and sent to a housing unit. Arriving there, I couldn't believe the huge steel structure covered in steel bars from floor to ceiling. I had never seen anything like it, not even in the movies. It was culture shock, I saw men from all over the world and heard many foreign languages. All nationalities and ethnic groups abounded.

There exists certain unwritten convict rules in prison and one of them is, you must hang with your own people. If you're from California, you hang with West Coast. If you're from New York, you hang with New York, or New Jersey, or even Philadelphia. It was like that. And in every group there's a Shot caller, to keep the order.

After several days on the Pound, word had spread about me and my homie, Capone. The New York crew introduced themselves. Believe this, they had already checked my history. They knew about me and my cases. The prison grapevine works very well and without interference. If someone ratted in his case, sooner or later, it could be found out, and I pity those who fall in that category.

Once I had settled in at one of the nation's most notorious prisons, I went straight to the law library and began the long and difficult task of trying to expose the government's wrongdoing and to secure my freedom.

Leavenworth's law library was relatively small compared to the one at Otisville, but that made no difference to me, because I was there for my "FREEDOM". I approached the counter for a request of some law books. There had been some cases I needed to check out that a friend of mine by name of Willie Graham, from Queens, New York had informed me, and might be of some assistance to me in my struggle to help win my "FREEDOM". Willie Graham was good at this craft of law, he had shown me some things that would help and assist me along the way as I began to mentally struggle for my "FREEDOM". I asked the law clerk for the books I wanted and he gave them to me. I went back and forth again and again for other books that led me back and forth to the law clerk counter. After several days in the law library, constantly requesting law books, the law clerk asked me, "where I was from" and I told him "Buffalo, New York." The law clerk said, "My Father went to trial in Buffalo, for something that had taken place in the Attica riot many years ago." I asked him "What was his Father's name?" and he said "Champ". I remember reading many years later on in life about the riot at Attica, New York, 45 minutes from Buffalo. I asked is your Father the guy that was the jail house lawyer that was on the inmate Attica panel requesting amnesty for the inmates. "Yeah! That's him!" I said I remembered seeing pictures of him in books. The next time I saw the law clerk, he showed me a picture of his father, and conveyed that he was from Bronx, New York and his name was Rob, and I told him my name is Sly Green, but they call my Stone as well. He said, "OH! The (Home Boys) told me about you Sly

14

Green," and he laughed and of course I laughed with him, and we became good friends.

For some reason after meeting Rob, I got the impression that he wanted to be a jail house lawyer, just like his Father Champ. Because Rob was good at it, and I had only known him for about 3½ years, I stayed in the law library at Leavenworth, and lived in it like when I had been at Otisville. I lived in it so much at Otisville, that the administration gave me a law clerk's job. I really studied hard and tried desperately to learn everything I could from Willie Graham, and anybody else, that I felt knew it. I even learned some things from Rob, because he was a very good researcher, but Willie Graham was a good writer too. I learned from them both, but I just couldn't write it then, I wasn't ready.   I didn't feel I could write it until years later at Colorado. Rob would be the one to mentally force me into learning how to write law and its language. It took at least six years for me to do my first case. When I did do it, I made sure I did everything I could to win. Otisville had been my start, and now I was at Leavenworth Federal United States Penitentiary.

When we got inside, it looked even worse, like the Morgue for dead people. When we got upstairs to the units, they were huge too, and extremely long like 80 cells long, three stories high, and two to a cell. I stayed on point and focused for at least a year, before the fear of just being in Leavenworth wore off me. All the stories I kept hearing about its past, the books I read on it, only made it worse for me. I said, *"Damn, I hope I don't catch a bodyup in this joint, because I am not going for nothing!"* But! Like I said, as time went on, I became less frightened about being there. Now, if that's not enough fear, when I went to the mess hall, I saw convicts from all over the world. You couldn't sit where you wanted to sit, you had to sit with your state or coast. Luckily, I was Sly Green, and it meant everything to me at that point. My name alone, saved me, it put me in high standings, with the East Coast Boys, especially from New York. I was that guy, a giant amongst other giants from the State of New York.

I was someone they respected and admired. Big Con had known me, and shown me great respect, he was the boss of the New York family there over both African Americans and Puerto Ricans. Big Con (Diaz) was from the Bronx, New York and I must say, he was extremely intelligent and very well respected by all the convicts in the entire prison. I hung with Big Con, and stayed close to the East Coast mob, as they became my family, and I became their family. We moved as one, on the orders from the "Don" Big Con.

I learned all I could about law, from any and whoever spoke it at Leavenworth. Mr. Skinner, was the genius of them all at Leavenworth, he was the main one of them all, but Rusty was good too, and so was Tommy Rutledge, and Shawn. I was transferred out of Leavenworth, for a fight. The winner went to a lower medium security prison and I was transferred to the worst Federal prison in the United States, even though I had lost the fight! The Administration had to have known, that if they let me out of the special housing, that I was going to straighten that guy from Waco, Texas, (Tony), whom one of his friends tripped me as I grabbed on to the Texas guy, and he ended up on top of me. I ended up out of the fight completely, but it was my first and only loss, and never did I ever lose another fight ever again. I held on to the notion for a very long time, that if I ever saw him again, we would definitely do a replay, but this time he was going to lose. However, I never saw him again, and I'm sure he was glad about that. I guess I can't win them all!

Leavenworth had been a very good learning experience, one that I would never ever forget. The food had been very good at Leavenworth, no complaints at all. The prison was vicious, and had constant murders, and stabbings, you simply had to be strong and mentally firm in your thoughts and real with yourself in order to survive Leavenworth. It was a very dangerous prison, and only the strong survived it.   PERIOD.   No question about it.

CHAPTER THREE

UNITED STATES HIGH SECURITY FEDERAL UNITED STATES PENITENTIARY AT FLORENCE, COLORADO

USP-Florence was among the newest, most high-tech and maximum security prisons in the United States. Known as the Alcatraz of the Rockies, it is just one of the jewels in the crown of the Bureau of Prison's Federal Correctional Complex at Florence, Colorado.

Set in a picturesque and tranquil valley of this south-central part of the state, danger and horror lurk within. It is no place for the timid and the weak.

This five star penitentiary is referred to as "the gang prison." Housed inside its massive concrete and steel walls live the leaders and members of some of this nation's most feared gang factions. Groups such as the Crips & Bloods, Gangster Disciples, Vice Lords, Surrenos, Dirty White Boys, Texas Syndicate, Mexican Mafia, Aryan Brotherhood, and many others to name a few. The gangs are prevalent in every segment of the prison population, a necessary evil that affords protection and commands respect for its members. Membership alone in one of these feared gangs, however, does not guarantee one's safety. Dangerous career criminals and psychopathic, paranoid schizophrenics blend into the mainstream of the prison population. Armed with homemade weapons, they are ready to lash out into a violent rage at any given moment. Stabbings occur with regularity and the murder rate is high. Staff couldn't protect you.

On the other side of these walls, only a stone's throw away, stands the infamous "ADX" or "Super

Max". It is the diamond in the BOP's crown of jewels. The ADX is unlike any prison that has ever come before it. No expense was spared in its construction. It possesses the most sophisticated and highly technical security measures ever implemented, because it is the lifetime residence of some of the most dangerous criminals the world has ever known.

Locked down twenty-four seven and permitted no physical contact with the outside, it's an existence that offers no hope. Any glimpse of the free world is a distant dream. Hell on earth resides at this address, and so did Donald Sly Green, if I violate any major prison rules in USP Florence High Security Penitentiary- right next door.

My journey to this wasteland began when I was placed aboard a BOP 727 prisoner transport plane. Handcuffed, shackled and chained, with the customary blackbox applied tight at the wrist, I settled into the window seat the U.S. Marshall had placed me in. This wasn't Southwest Airlines, so you sit wherever the Marshall so directs, but your luggage does travel free. Looking out the window I wondered how all of this could be happening and what the future held, but there were no answers.

When finally the plane landed at some remote country airport, the name Donald Green was called and I slowly rose from my seat and moved to the rear of the plane and descended the stairs. I squinted from the blinding light of the bright sunshine and then saw all the Marshalls and other Federal law enforcement agents and correctional officers standing in a circle armed with automatic shotguns and M-16's at the ready. There were transport buses from all the Federal agencies and the Bureau of Prisons, all lined strategically side by side. I was directed to the BOP-Florence bus, as were a number of others. I found an empty window seat and sat down. Looking around, I counted forty prisoners in all. The bus began to roll and this unforgettable journey was now in its final stage. The trip from the airport was approximately thirty-five miles of unincorporated roadways. All I saw were livestock fences and horses grazing and the majestic peaks of the Rockies off in the distance. They were a beautiful and imposing sight.

When the bus arrived at the huge Federal complex, over half of the prisoners demanded protective custody status, fearing of what horrors may await them in the general population. I was not one known to be soft and though somewhat apprehensive about the unknown, I was prepared to meet my destiny head-on and without any hesitation. I went straight to the compound.

Without handcuffs or other constraints and wearing a fresh set of bus clothes, I walked slowly toward the housing unit to which staff had directed me. Out of nowhere I heard someone yell my name. When I turned, I saw several familiar faces. There were several of the guys I had met during my time at Leavenworth, even one I remembered from Otisville. I stopped to greet them but was hurried along by a guard who told me to keep moving and then chased the others. Seeing these familiar faces caused me to relax a little, though I still kept my awareness level high, constantly on the alert and watching my back, because it was required here in this belly of the beast.

After several weeks, I discovered that USP-Florence was everything I had heard about the place. It was both ruthless and dangerous, a battle zone with gangs fighting and killing each other.

I couldn't make any sense of this caveman mentality that pitted inmate against inmate, and it saddened me deeply. I wondered why these various gang factions didn't band together to achieve common goals such as improving their environment. Take the food, for example. It was atrocious, barely fit to eat. But, they did nothing and just ate the dogfood that was fed to them. The only thing that kept me from falling victim to this mentality was the law library. I would spend the majority of my time there, still learning as I researched the complex legal issues of my case. I found it unbelievable that here in this modern day, super maximum security dungeon of some seventeen hundred inmates, barely one hundred would utilize the tools in the law library to make a challenge to their convictions and sentences. Many of the inmates were serving multiple life sentences. Why wouldn't they want to learn about the law and see if they could help themselves? Why wouldn't they consult with the other inmates or law clerks and ask questions or have them explain any issues they might have regarding the specific facts of their cases and, if there were any, to challenge them?

Make no mistake, many a Federal case have been won by inmates defending themselves and others. Inmates taught themselves the law through long and arduous studies and applied that learning in their endeavor to obtain freedom. The Federal cite books – the Federal Supplement, the Fed. Second and Fed. Third, Lawyer's Editions, the entire gamut, are all filled with examples of cases that have been overturned and won at every Federal judicial level, all the way to the United States Supreme Court.

It would not be very long before I had the convictions and sentences I was responsible for overturning and winning appear in these very same legal volumes. I was determined to learn as much about the law as I could. It was my only ticket out of this madness and captivity. I spent all of my free time reading and learning. I would even stop work on my own case and readily assist others with theirs. I gave freely of my time and the legal knowledge I was quickly accumulating. I swore I would never assist any inmate who had cooperated with the government, not under any circumstances, and this was well known throughout the prison. If you had cooperated with the government and testified against another, do not bring your case to me because I would not accept it.

And so, the diaries of a jailhouse lawyer continue.

CHAPTER FOUR

LEWISBURG, PENNSYLVANIA
UNITED STATES FEDERAL PENITENTIARY

Lewisburg Federal Penitentiary at Lewisburg, Pennsylvania, was built around 1932. The prison was a statement of penological dignity, self-esteem, and power, if you believe the designer of Lewisburg, Alfred Hopkins (1870-1941), who stated that Lewisburg was one of the most significant architects of American prisons.

He was also a prison reformer who believed that when all was said and done, there was little difference between convicts and other people. Good architecture, he thought, would have its effect on both the convicts and the custodial staff, whom it might inspire to become "wise" and "tolerant". Hopkins wanted to create a world that was both aesthetically gratifying and morally useful. He therefore, wanted Lewisburg to be "forceful", "fitting", and even "pleasant" in its "mood".

At Lewisburg, he built the windows small and put bars on the inside rather than the outside, to maintain the institution's Renaissance appearance from the outside. The inside view was different: the windows were indeed small, and the bars sticking out from them constantly reminded an inmate that he was a convict living in a prison cell. Whether it be despite or because of its architect's seeming self-assurance, Lewisburg, was an important architectural statement, but what it said to inmates was different from what it said to its architect.

Lewisburg, from an inmate's perspective was a very dangerous Federal prison, it was known very well throughout the Federal system for its murders, drugs, stabbings, killing snitches, taking advantage of the weak, and lots of knife play. It had a metal shop where the inmates made their own weapons of choice in steel. You had to be a very standup guy to make it through Lewisburg, or you would never survive it, not even for a day, because the inmates had basically control of the prison. They murdered, and killed and stabbed and injured each other at will. Each of the Federal Penitentiaries I went to, I would learn that they all had one specific thing they did not tolerate, or was known for and at Lewisburg, it seemed to be for controlling the prison by the inmates. They were in control of the joint, no question about it. But, as you read on in this book, you'll come to the realization that it's not a good thing when inmates are in control of a prison, you'll see why I make such a statement.

Anyway, the cells in Lewisburg were extremely HOT in the winter and summer. With no air conditioning, we constantly overheated at Lewisburg, but the law library was the first place Dakim from the Bronx took me to when I stepped in the joint. Dakim was a cool, smooth dude, very respectful and extremely real. Dakim was a five percenter, it was his culture. He believed strongly in his African American Brothers, and was a very uplifting brother. I meant it when I said he was real to the death. Dakim was my partner at Lewisburg, plus we had been together at a state joint when I was younger, called Elmira, New York, and he had already impressed me with his seriousness and gentlemanly respect for his race. After he took me to the law library, I looked around the spot and it was very BIG, and had a lot of books that other Federal prisons I had been to did not have.

I got right into my case, and developed a relationship with the law clerks, and other inmates who were constantly doing research. I had already been in prison for over ten (10) years when I hit Lewisburg, and had learned all of the basic things I needed to learn about the Federal law, but there was so much more I had to learn, if I was ever to be released from Federal custody. I was serving four (4) life terms, plus 110 years for the Federal sentence, plus 25 years to life for the State of New York. I couldn't see the light, because there was none. I couldn't see through the tunnel, because there was no light to guide me through. I had to create a whole new world and make my own light, if I was ever to be released. That would definitely, with no doubt, have to come from research, constant reading, constant law questions, and thousands of hours in the law library.

It would take years, if not the rest of my entire life, to get my freedom, if I was ever to be released from the FEDS. They simply did not follow their own rules at times. They would arrest your entire family, and go all over the world and find a witness to testify against you. Simply put! They would do any and everything within their power to take you down, to win a case. This was not the State. This was the most powerful government in the world that I was up against and I was no match for them, but I stayed on top of my case. I stayed in the law library and I was not about to give up under any circumstances at all.

I had gone through two very serious trials, both state and Federal. In the State trial I had been lied on by a witness, Mr. James Wright, and a guy by the name of Steven Brown. I had never in my life, seen either of the two, yet here they were testifying against me. Mr. Wright for $250,000.00 dollars, and Steven Brown, for a pending case he had against him. The State knew both of them were lying, but it was Donald Sly Green, the name alone, that forced them to pay whatever was asked in order to send an innocent man away for 25 years to life. Even the Judge, was on the side of the prosecution. I had the best defense money could afford, but sometimes even money can't save an innocent individual.

I continued to research the New York State case, but I was unable to do good solid research, because the Feds did not carry New York State legal material, and when I would write to Albany, New York for it, to the New York State Department of Corrections, they would not send me any of the requested information. When I wrote to the Attorney General, complaining about a lack of New York State legal material, I received the same result. No response. I was stuck. I had to make due with whatever New York State legal material I bought or ran across.

As I got to know the regular guys, who attended the law library, like (ICE) Walter Cook, Tommy Walker Mr. Burnell Gibson, and others (I can't remember all of them), we would sit in groups and speak of the cases that we had run across, and/or were researching, in the event they might be of some benefit to one of us. We did this usually at least once a day, and we usually tried to stay in there as much as we could, researching and learning law.

My opinion is that, at that time, Tommy Walker, was the best, though others felt Meka was the best jailhouse lawyer, at that time in Lewisburg. But little did either of the two know I was learning, reading, and researching all I could, so that one day I too, could be called one of the Best, and or in the top ten in the Federal system.

While at Lewisburg, I received a win on my Title 28 U.S.C. Section 2255 Motion, the government had tried to stop me from being able to file it, because they felt I had filed it late, I felt I had not, and so with the help of my jailhouse lawyer friends from USP-Colorado, I contested everything the government said in its attempt to stop me from pursuing my Section 2255 Motion issues. It took from 1997 to July of 2000 for the government to lose on Appeal. I was in Lewisburg when I received the order from the U.S. Court of Appeals for the Second Circuit. Of course, I was radiant and very happy. Now I could present all of my issues and some more, and I no longer trusted in lawyers like I had in the past. I wanted to win for myself, and along with the help and research of other inmates, and then request counsel, if I won. It had taken me approximately six years to learn what I was doing in law, and how to write it and research it. I had won my very first case in USP-Florence, Colorado, for a guy from Philly, PA. It was a misdemeanor case, I filed a speedy trial motion for him on the case, and months later, they dismissed the case. Another guy at Florence, from South Carolina, had probation violations. I sent letters to all of the probation people explaining how he was working in the prison, taking advantage of all the necessary programs available to him, and how he was trying to rehabilitate himself, so that upon re-entry back into society he would be a more productive member of society upon his re-entry. South Carolina said nothing the first few months and I continued on with the letters every time this inmate achieved and or made more progress. About eight months later, South Carolina suspended his probation time that he had left. I took another case. It was a Title 21 U.S.C. Section 848(b) case, a Super Kingpin case. Some inmates, don't like people to put their names in books. So we'll call him Kiko. He was from California. He was a Crip gang member and he asked for my legal assistance, and I said let me see what it is first. I looked it over, and informed him. I let him know if there was anything I could do on the case. A few days later I got back with Kiko, and told him I had an 848 as well, and that I wanted to do three issues on the case. It took me several months, and when I gave him the three issues all typed up and ready to go, he sent them to his lawyer, who was doing a Writ of Certiorari for him, and she asked him "Who did this for you- it's very good." She used it, and Kiko was sent back to the Seventh Circuit U.S. Court of Appeals, about his 848, which stated that the 848(b) carried a mandatory life sentence without release, unless he won in court, the 848(a) carried 20 years to life, but Kiko had been charged with just 848, with the penalty phrase, and given no penalty subdivision of (a) or (b). I saw it, and did an issue on it, and two other issues on something else in the case, but Kiko won on the 848 issue, and he wrote to me several years later through another inmate and thanked me with all of his heart for what I had done for him.   One day in my researching of new cases, I had seen the case, and Kiko was now in the Seventh Circuit.   I was happy for him, and so when I received the letter from him, I felt power and confidence in myself and that I could do this law thing. It made me strive harder.   It made me know that if I could do it for others, I damn sure could win my own. I thought back to Otisville, and then to Leavenworth, where I had met Mase, briefly, who also would become a great jailhouse lawyer. Years later when I would meet up with him again in Coleman, Florida, a Federal prison complex. I thought of the guy Leon from St. Louis, Missouri, who was serving a Federal sentence, and waiting to be sent to the state after the completion of his Federal sentence of 83 years. Leon had been the one in Colorado, whom had said to me "Stone, you do very good research, but you have to learn to write the law and use its language. Let me see when you write up issues, and when you get it, I'll let you know when you've learned to write law." I wrote and wrote for approximately two years or more until one day Leon said, "You've got it pal," and I was like "Are you for real, you serious? I got it, for real Leon." He said, "One day, you'll be one of the best that ever did it." When he left Colorado to go to Missouri State prison system, he too left me a letter telling me that I was destined to be a great jailhouse lawyer, and that I had what it took to win cases. Of course, I believed him, of course I was overwhelmed with happiness, and I said to myself, there's no way I'm staying for five life terms, plus 135 years in prison.

I studied harder now. I took on a few more cases and went to Lewisburg. These are the things I thought of when I flashed and reminisced back into the past. I thought back again to my friend Rick Turkorse, a lawyer out of Atlanta, Georgia, who was at Colorado with me, he only stayed briefly, but for the few months that he did stay, I learned all I could from him. Rick was cool, and taught law classes at Florence High Security Colorado, and I didn't miss one class of his. He left about eight months or so later, and I never saw him again. I was told he went to a medium security prison in Oregon, near California.

These are the things I would think about whenever I won cases. These flash backs, kept me focused, kept me thinking and wanting my freedom, and pushed me to where I am mentally today.

I must admit that I am grateful and now humbled by the fact that I had to stand strong and firm, in order to get to where I am today, which is aware of my circumstances and the sub-human conditions I endure in prison every single day. The fact is that I may never ever be released, but I must try any way and stay fighting to the death. Because if I ever gave up, I'll die that day, because I'll have given up the fight to fight for my "FREEDOM". Believe me, I am truly mindful of the sacrifices I had to make with me being incarcerated. I know my two sons and daughter say to themselves - why Daddy? And I say to myself, it was the life I lived at that time and era. If I never ever get free, it won't ever be because I was not trying also, because I stayed focused and in that law library. The challenges I have faced in these prisons are many, jealousy, fabrications, misunderstandings, stumbling blocks of all kinds, and hurdles that I had to get around in order to stay on my case and in the law library. I have to be the Best of the best in jail house lawyers, in order to win on five life terms, plus 135 years in Federal and State prisons. I must succeed or else I will die in here without ever being released. Therefore, even at Lewisburg, I studied hard. I watched and learned all I could from all of the other jail house lawyers in Lewisburg, because I was searching for something to help me win my own case. Therefore, I knew I could never crumble under pressure of any kind or fall into any type of mental or spiritual ruin, because if I did, my life and dream of "FREEDOM would surely be over. So there could never, ever be any calamities or crisis with myself or about myself, nor would I ever go to war against myself. Everything I did and said while in these prisons would be to the benefit of gaining my "FREEDOM". I just couldn't look at it realistically any other way. These are the things I reflected on when I won a case, or an issue. I simply had to stay in a very positive and realistic state of mind. If I was ever to be "FREE".

CHAPTER FIVE

SCHYULKILL FCI, PENNSYLVANIA

I had been incarcerated from 1989 to 2002, when I was transferred to Schyulkill F.C.I. in Pennsylvania. The Warden of Lewisburg, a Mr. Scott Didrull, allowed me a golden opportunity to transfer to a Federal Correctional Facility, rather than stay in a United States Penitentiary for the rest of my life. I must admit that I was grateful for this golden opportunity he was bestowing upon me. Mr. Didrull asked me how long had I been incarcerated and I told him over ten years in a Federal Penitentiary. He then asked me when was the last time I had a disciplinary report, and I said over five years ago. He then asked what was I incarcerated for, and I said the Super Kingpin Act, Title 21 U.S.C. Section 848, RICO Enterprise, 18 U.S.C. Section 1962-1963, Conspiracy, Title 21 U.S.C. Section 846, and multi drug charges, but I went to trial. I also stated that I had a New York State case I was serving time for as well. Mr. Didrull requested that I come and see him in a week back there in the mess hall. It was during the noon meal, while all staff and inmates alike are in the front of the mess hall entrance that you can talk to the staff about anything- health, doctors, nurses, etc. Some of everybody is in there, and they were very professional, and did their jobs well. That's my opinion. Other convicts will differ with me on that statement for reasons of their own. Well, I went back a week later, and I saw the Warden, and Mr. Seitzit, the Assistant Warden, who was with him, holding his four fingers up, so I could see them. I said Mr. Seitzit I know I have 4 life terms, plus 110 years, and 25-to-life for the State of New

York, and Mr. Seitzit stated that he'd transfer me because I'd been doing very well, and I said, "Thank You" to the Warden and it was truly one of the happiest days in my entire life. I was so happy, I didn't tell anyone, but Dakim, and Big Koola, and of course they didn't believe I was going anywhere, but a few months later in April of 2002, I left USP Lewisburg, never ever did I want to see another Federal Penitentiary ever again. It was too much violence, too many stabbings, too many murders, and too many conflicts with each other (other inmates) all the time. I didn't want to be in a shot caller position, I knew what that meant, constant problems, constant leadership, constant advice, constant this and constant that. I would never be able to get any law work done, if I ever accepted a position like that. So I stayed in the background, while Dakim, Big Pope, May-May, and the other O.G.'s called the shots. I was usually with Big Koola, though because he was very intelligent, smooth, cool, but very serious, dangerous, and one of the top bosses from Washington, D.C. Big Koola, plain and simple, was the truth and we were in the same unit. We went mostly everywhere together, we were truly the Best of Friends, but I wanted out of those violent and very dangerous penitentiaries. Because like I said, they killed each other too much, they hurt each other too much, and they were simply self-destructing. You would never be able to get a lot of law work done, because you would be locked down months at a time, if not for this, then for that.

I wanted to win my case. I wanted as much time as possible in that law library without being locked down all the time for one thing or another. So I was transferred to Schyulkill, Pennsylvania F.C.I. When I got there I was the happiest guy in the world. I honestly could not believe I was that guy whom had traveled back and forth at times on a U.S. military helicopter to court and went to trial with over 150 U.S. Marshalls outside the court, and inside the court, with U.S. Marshall's blocking the streets, and areas around the Court House off for a three mile radius, snipers on all the surrounding buildings, F.B.I. Agents at all the bus-stops, Federal Agents and U.S. Marshalls everywhere. This was for months, while I was on trial. I couldn't believe that I was there, and that I did not have to wear the Black Box on my handcuffs anymore. It was all over for those days, it had taken from 1989 to 2002 for all of that to stop. I had no intentions of ever allowing myself to ever be subjected to that type of brutal and harsh treatment ever again if I had anything to do with it. So when I got to Schyulkill, I went straight to the law library. It was my first stop of course, I wanted to see what it looked like, what was it, how it was run, and who was working in it. There were a lot of guys from New York City there, along with Boston, Philly, Delaware, Washington, D.C., Connecticut, Maryland, Virginia, North Carolina, and many other states. They had heard the name Sly Green for a long time, but I didn't know it. I had been isolated in those penitentiaries throughout the United States, Leavenworth, Colorado, Lewisburg, and now a F.C.I. So there were about 50 or more guys whom introduced themselves to me, and I was happy to know that they knew of me, and respected me so highly. They were from everywhere too. There was Tu-Quan, Gotti Johnson, Inch, Big Scoop, Jughead, Stacy, BeBo, and Science- too many to name. We all talked, and I thanked them all for their respect and walked the yard with them until it was time to go back to the units that evening. It was simply a good start. I even met Kevin Kelly from

New York, a guy from the Westies, an Irish organization from New York City. Kevin Kelly was highly respected throughout the Federal system. He was a real gentleman, and a real stand-up guy. I liked and respected him as such. There were a lot of mob guys there. They were cool and serious too, and they demanded their respect, and they got it.

The next day, I went to the law library until I got a job, which was cleaning the compound, for a few months. I got a job in the school, working for the pre-release center for Ms. Kay. She was a very nice and very intelligent lady. I just couldn't understand how such a very pretty, and intelligent lady could be working in a Federal prison as a pre-release supervisor, but here she was, there at Schyulkill F.C.I. every day for work. She was my boss, until I got another job in the recreation area, but I stayed in the law library. I stayed working out, lifting weights, and doing pull ups, pushups and dips. The law library was where I lived almost all of my time. I became good friends with a guy by the name of Big Scoop from Yonkers, New York, and he was lifting over five hundred pounds on the bench. He worked out constantly. He was the Young General Boss of the New York car. He ruled the team with an intelligent way of thinking. He was a real gentleman gangster. There was absolutely nothing bad or negative about Big Scoop, he was the realest, youngest, General I had thus far ever encountered that knew how to move and when to move, and how to use his soldiers. There was Tu-Quan too from Brooklyn, New York. He was real too, and Gotti Johnson, and Science, they too were real and Stacy and Broadway too. But, I must confess, that Big Scoop was the realest of them all, and then came Jughead from Queens. They moved when Big Scoop spoke, and if he was not present, then Jughead had the spot. Then there was Big King, Darnell King from Mount Vernon, New York. He was a con man, a very big guy in size, shrewd, and wise.

When I saw Miles at Lewisburg from Yonkers, I asked him, did he know Big Scoop, and he said he'd heard that name several times. I said all the rappers from Yonkers usually gave Big Scoop a shot out internationally. But Miles had only heard the name. I hung regularly with these guys at Schyulkill. I met a few guys from Buffalo, like my homeboy Keppie. He was cool and we kicked it around often until he went home about a year later. Also there were a few more from Buffalo, Rochester, Syracuse, and Albany, New York. Other guys came through and I kicked it with them, but Big Scoop, Tu-Quan, Gotti Johnson, and Big King were the ones I was very close with. There were some guys from Lewisburg in Schyulkill too, and they must have put the word out that I was into the legal work, doing law, that it was something I was always doing, so within a few months I started taking cases, looking at them, to see if I should or should not take them, or if I could win them or not. I remember the first case I took for a guy. We'll call him Mexico, because that's what I really called him by.

He had been arrested for meth, cocaine, and marijuana, and given a 30 year sentence in Atlanta, Georgia. I took the case, based on a Title 28 U.S.C. Section 2255 motion. But he had already had another inmate whom had already submitted the Section 2255 motion, but that inmate was in lock-down, for tricking and scheming on other inmates for their legal fees, as if he knew the law, although he did not know anything at all about the law. He was simply a con man, scheming on as many inmates as he could to get their money until they realized that he was a fake and a fraud. That is when they checked him into the Special Housing Unit. I supplemented to the case, on several occasions, and approximately 13 months later, Mexico was called to the Northern District of Georgia for a hearing. He was the first win I had at Schyulkill, I was happy for the win, and I would go on to win 13 more cases, based on drugs and guns. I was growing to love everything about criminal law. I was a constant resident of that law library, it was my home now. It was my only way to "FREEDOM". I could even go on Sunday mornings from 7:30 a.m. all the way to 3:00 P.M. I could dam near stay all day on the weekends. I was loving it. The second case I took was a case from a Chinese guy, he was a major heroin trafficker, and we will call him China. He was in my unit, B-2, with me and one day he sent another Chinese guy to me, to ask if I would work on his case. I said let me see what it's about first and I'll let you know if I can do anything with it. A few days later, I spoke again to the Chinese guy, and to the one that did not speak any English, or very little English. I took the transcripts and looked over the case. I realized from the start of my reading the case that China, like myself, had already been incarcerated for over 10 years, had been affirmed on all of his appeals. There was only one way in which I felt would work and that was to go through a Civil Procedure Rule 60(B)(6). So I told him what I felt about the case, it was a very big heroin case, out of Chicago, Illinois, in the very early 1990's. Probably the biggest one ever there at that time. I took the case, and I pulled Big King (Darnell King) in on the case with me. We worked on the case together for about nine months or so. We put in the 60(B)(6), based on the integrity of the proceedings that had taken place in the case. We waited for a response, which took about 60 or so days for the District Court to respond. I had challenged the fact that China had received a 25 year sentence in violation of his statutory maximum that exceeded a sentence allowed by the U.S. Congress and the Statute. Because China had been charged with Title 21 U.S.C. Section 841 (a)(1), not (b)(1)(B), nor (b)(1)(A), which both carried mandatory minimums, China should have received no more than a 20 year sentence at most, not 25 years. I felt the court had used the wrong integrity of the proceedings to sentence China. I also felt that his Fifth Amendment rights to due process and Sixth Amendment rights to a beyond a reasonable doubt had been violated, because he should have received no more than 20 years at most. I felt that his Eighth Amendment rights to cruel and unusual punishment had also been a factor, and I challenged the integrity of the proceedings in regards to how China had been unconstitutionally sentenced and the fact that the jury had never been instructed on Title 21 U.S.C. Section 841(b)(1)(B), nor (b)(1)(A), which carried mandatory minimums, but not Section 841(a)(1). The government was told it had 30 days to respond, and when that 30 days was up, they wanted 30 more and of course they got it as usual when they make such requests. The government had stated that China's Fifth, Sixth, and Eighth Amendment rights had not been violated, and that the wrong integrity of proceedings had not been used, and that the Movant should have brought this issue up in a Section 2255 motion for which he had already exhausted. And that Movant had been enhanced through a preponderance of evidence, within his U.S.S. Guideline range. And that Movant's case had no merit to it and that the court had no jurisdiction to hear Movant's

Civil Procedure Rule 60(b)(6). This was the government's response. Of course, I responded back and stated I reassert, affirm and reaffirm all the original information in my already submitted claim, and that I do not concede to the government. Approximately several months later, I lost the case and wanted to appeal it, but China didn't want to appeal. He preferred not to, and so I let it go. A few weeks after that I was given another Chinese case from New York in the Southern District of New York, and it too was a major drug case. But this guy spoke very good English, and we communicated very well. His was a 2255 Motion/ Petition/ Memorandum of Law case. Counsel had not appealed, upon the petitioner's request to do so, and counsel had not called the witnesses that petitioner wanted called. There had been an illegal search and seizure issue that counsel had not pursued when he should have. Counsel had prejudiced the petitioner by not pursuing these issues, and caused the petitioner 30 years in a Federal prison. I accused counsel of ineffective assistance of counsel, below the standards of representation, and stated that counsel should have appealed upon the petitioner's request to do so. I stated that counsel should have called the petitioner's witnesses he wanted called and why he should have called them. I stated in the Section 2255 Motion that the search had been illegal because those officers were not given permission to enter into that apartment in Chinatown, and that they forced their way in without exigent circumstances, and without the occupant's permission, I stated how the search was an illegal search and seizure in violation of the petitioner's Fourth Amendment rights to illegal search and seizure. I constantly accused counsel of prejudice and stated because of the fact that the petitioner wanted to appeal his 30 year plea, that counsel had a Sixth Amendment duty to appeal his case on direct appeal review. I quoted Roe v. Ortga, 528 U.S. 470 (2000); Strickland v. Washington, 466 U.S. 668-687 (1984); Cronic v. United States, 466 U.S. 648 (1984); Glover v. United States, 531 U.S. 198-203 (2001); Hill v. Lockhart, 474 U.S. 52 (1985). I stated how had it not been for counsel's ineffectiveness and below the standard of representation, petitioner would never have received 30 years, but would have proceeded directly to trial. I explained that petitioner's plea was an involuntary, unintelligent, and unknowing, and that had the petitioner known that counsel was leading him, and ill-advising him, that he would have never pled guilty and instead would have proceeded to trial.

I sent it all in and I waited on the government to respond. When they did, because the Judge told them to, they said the usual things they always say, which is petitioner's Section 2255 Motion is frivolous without merit, and false allegations, etc. Then I hit back once again with a few new cases, and stayed on counsel's unprofessionalism as a counsel guaranteed to the petitioner by the Sixth Amendment of the United States Constitution. Had I known all of this and that counsel was misguiding and ill-advising the petitioner, he would have removed counsel off of his case with the permission of the court, due to of all of this prejudice that petitioner's plea was involuntary, unintelligent, and unknowingly. I waited for the Judge to give the final opinion and/or order. About seven months later, I won the Chinese guy an Evidentiary Hearing. Of course, I was happy for him. But, at the very same time, I was saying to myself, that I've got to do this for myself as well. I started to focus on my own case as well, looking and trying to find any and everything that would help me. I went on in Schyulkill to win 3 cases, but with the "<u>Firm</u>", that Big King had initiated. It happened like this: One day while at a lunch meal in the mess hall, in Schyulkill, Pennsylvania, myself and Big King and a guy from Syracuse, named "Truth", were sitting together eating, I asked Truth out of curiosity where he was from, and he said Syracuse, New York. I stated to him I knew some people up there, and I asked him did he know Ronnie Moore, Big O'Dee, Big Red, May-May, Comer, and some other guys. He either knew them or had heard of them. He knew some people out of Buffalo, none that I knew, and we kicked it and became friends afterwards. He asked me my name at the table and I said Sly Green, but they call me Stone too. He said he'd heard a lot of good things about Sly Green. He started talking about what he had heard and things of that nature, and Big King overheard him, but I stopped Truth, before he said too much. Big King was on the prowl now. I would realize it was too late, because a few days later, Big King and I started talking in the law library and we became the best of friends. A few months later, Big King, whom studied law as well, said, "Yo! Stone! Let's put a firm together". So we got a typist, a researcher, along with myself and Big King. That's how we became "The Firm" from that day on. Big King would always come up with better ways to improve the Firm, for instance, by insisting that we always listen to the defendant's story and what they have to say, and always pay attention to what's being said to you from the client. You don't have to believe them, but at least listen to what they have to say. So we hired a writer, to write any and everything we felt was important whenever we interviewed a client. As time went on, we had to hire three typists, 3 researchers, and I had a writer as well as Big King had a writer, we both had so much work to do including working on our own cases, that law work and our physical exercises was all that mattered. We took the Schyulkill spot over completely with the law. When Big-E from Washington, D.C. came, we felt he would be the perfect guy to leave all of our clients with when we left to go to Bennettsville, South Carolina F.C.I. We left all of the Clients with Big-E because he too was the real deal in law, and was very sincere and trustful. Schyulkill was my first real test of how the firm could win cases. We won a total of 13 cases at Schyulkill. Big King had been the one to show me though that I needed help, plenty of help, to win cases, and that there was no way we could win all those cases just by ourselves. When we hit Bennettsville, South Carolina together, we created another firm, with Big King always running the firm. Run it he did, he was a very good boss too. When we touched down in Bennettsville, we interviewed guys for a job in the firm. Our name was good with the names. Big King used the motto, one finger to the left side of the chest, firm! From there we started blowing up, but within about three months after being there, the administration transferred me. Some inmate told the administration that he was afraid I was going to do something to him, because of his Father, whom had told his son over a phone call, to go to the authorities and tell them who his Father was, and that he could not be around me because if I discovered who his Father was, I might do something to his son. Even though I would have never done anything like that I was placed in the Special Housing Unit and transferred within sixty days after being placed in the Special Housing Unit. Big King kept the firm going though, and when I was transferred to Atlanta USP, in Atlanta, Georgia, I put a firm together there. I told them all about Big King and that wherever they go, create a firm and it's the left finger up to the chest with YO! Firm! Firm! FAMILY!!

CHAPTER SIX

ATLANTA USP

Atlanta USP looked just like Lewisburg and Leavenworth USP's. All three of them put you through the ultimate test of who you really are, in the sense that you question whether or not you can survive in places like this. Just looking at them, puts the fear of God in you. When you go inside them, it is even worse, because of those long hallways, the cells, the place- period. They looked exactly like what they were, United States Penitentiaries. All three of them were some serious Joints and don't let anyone fool you or tell you anything different. You had to stand strong in those joints or you would not survive. They were no place for the timid nor the weak. Those convicts would eat the timid and the weak alive if they saw just the slightest sign of weakness. That did happen a lot in those places and often too. Honestly, I was glad my name was Sly Green.   I was proud to be who I was and make no mistake about it, I had fights and very serious situations, but I only lost one of them, and that was in Leavenworth, Kansas. After that incident I never saw him again to straighten it out, because they transferred him before I could get to him and they transferred me first before him. After that I never ever came close to a loss. I kept it completely gangster when necessary, which was most of the time in those USP's. It was mandatory. None of them were as worse and dangerous as USP High Security Colorado, in Florence, Colorado. It was truly a very dangerous and vicious joint. I held my own completely and kept it gangster.

In Atlanta, my job was working as a law clerk. A

white guy by the name of Crooker, from South Carolina, got me the job. He told me he had heard some very positive and good things about me. He asked me did I want the job. I said YES! Of course, I wanted a law library job. I was in there 3 days later after my orientation process which every inmate has to attend. Once in the law library, I would usually stay all day except for the two hours I used for working out and trying to keep my body in shape. I felt it extremely necessary to stay in physical shape in order to be able to stay in shape mentally. Anyway, it was a must for me to stay in shape in the penitentiary, because you never knew what was going to happen from day to day in those places; so working out was a must, even mandatory.

About a year after I was in Atlanta, my good friend the Young General, Big Scoop came in with a few other homeboys from the East Coast - T.L. (Tony Long from Philly), a black Mafia Captain from Philly; 50 from the Bronx, and his partner Ja, Kobini Savage from Philly, a young gangster; Castro from Reading, Pennsylvania, who was all about learning the law; Dog from Washington, D.C., who was my good friend too. I was very happy to see Big Smity again, who took a bust in Buffalo, New York; another good friend, Ben-Gee from Boston; Ike from Buffalo; West from Buffalo; and many others. Altogether it was at least about 52 of us there that hung together every single day. Big Scoop, the Young General, kept the East Coast family in check, in physical shape, and on top as well as T.L. and Big Ya-Ya, from Brooklyn and Dee from Harlem. I had not seen unity like this in a while, since Leavenworth with Big Con (Diaz) from the Bronx. The East Coast unity was crazy, cool, and family for real, but it was all because of T.L. and the Young General, Big Scoop, and YES Ya-Ya too.   He kept it strong as well. We had power in Atlanta, influence, and was the top car in that joint, no question about it. Most of my homeboys would come to the law library, because Big Scoop, the General and T.L. wanted all paperwork checked to see if everything was cool, or not cool, so I checked the ones they sent to me, and they were all "Frosty" (Cool). Whenever any of my homeboys needed legal work done, myself, Castro, and the firm did it for free. Yes, we put a firm together even in Atlanta. Big King had taught me well on how to put a firm together and I stayed in touch with Big King while he was at Bennettsville with always the first words, YO! Firm up! I loved my friend Big King, the Young General, and Dog from D.C. like they were my real brothers, because I never met guys like them in my life, and T.L. was cool too!

Atlanta's Law library was the best one I liked, because Mr. Jones, the supervisor, made sure I was able to research any and every case, they came out with if I asked for it, or could identify it. Mr. Jones was the law library supervisor, and he was real cool, but so was Mr. Shewder, who was our supervisor too. Ms. Ford, who worked in the Education Department with Ms. Coleman, were very nice African American people. I must admit, Ms. Ford, was a very pretty lady to be working in a Federal United States Penitentiary. You could not keep your eyes off of that pretty lady. Anyway, I loved that law library. I stayed focused on reading every and anything about law. I had grown to love it and everything about it. It was no longer hard for me to comprehend it like I used to have to understand it over and over again. I just could not go a day without some law- reading it, writing it, or learning about a new case. Crooker was cool and I thanked him for the job. I really appreciated it too.

One day about a year after being in Atlanta, Crooker got into a verbal altercation with a Lt. there, and they locked him up. I never ever saw him ever again. Months later, they transferred Crooker. Me, Castro, and Big 86, from West Palm Beach, Florida, and a bank robber from Atlanta, Georgia, held it down from there. Me and Castro continued to build the firm, and made it strong as best as we could. It was in Atlanta that I took my first Atlanta case, from an Asian guy, from Tampa, Florida. He had not filed an appeal, but stated that his counsel told him he had no appeal rights, because he had pled guilty. I asked him how long he had been in prison, when he was sentenced. He told me his one year time limitation was not yet up for the filing of a Section 2255 motion. I asked him about his guideline points. I asked him how much time he had, and he told me and showed me his presentence report. I asked him many more questions, and he answered them, so I filed a Section 2255 motion for him, based on ineffective assistance of counsel in violation of his Sixth Amendment rights to a direct appeal. I stated that counsel had prejudiced the Asian guy, by refusing to pursue a direct appeal, upon the Asian guy's request to file one. I challenged some of the points he had received for both a gun, and a separate sentence for the gun as well. I challenged his drug amount, based on the relevant conduct he received that caused him to be enhanced, based on a preponderance of the evidence.

I put it together, and gave the researcher some cases to look up, after that I wrote it up and put it together. I gave it to Castro to see if I had left anything misspelled or out because <u>Gomez-Diaz v. United States,</u> 433 F.3d 788-793 (2005)(11th Cir.), had just come out;

Roe v. Ortega, 528 U.S. 470 (2000), I used. I hit them with Hill v. Lockhart, 474 U.S. 52 (1985); Strickland v. Washington, 466 U.S. 668-687 (1985); Cronic v. United States, 466 U.S. 648 (1984); and I told the courts that there was no way that the Petitioner was supposed to have received a 60 month sentence for the gun possession and a 2 point enhancement for it. I told the court that the Asian guy had a Sixth Amendment right to a direct appeal and that counsel had a duty to file it upon request of the petitioner.

I gave it to the Asian guy and told him to make copies on the copy machine, making one for the court, one for the U.S. Attorney's Office, and keep one for himself. I then told him put them in two brown envelopes, but sign them in two places, and send the two envelopes out in the morning. He did! I waited for a few months. The courts told the government to respond within sixty days. The government, as usual, requested an extension, and they got it. I waited for the sixty days and the government responded and I pushed on. I put it on them, because I had a 24 hour a day job, the law library. I loved what I did.   I loved law, as it was mental food to me. It was great to me. I wanted nothing more than to win, win, and win; and I did win and I did send the Asian guy back to the Middle District of Florida, the Tampa Division. He never did anything I told him to do, once he got back, he didn't listen to any of my mock Evidentiary Hearings that I and Castro and the others in The Firm put him through. He must have thought it was a game, and so when I spoke to him after he had come back empty handed without winning any of the issues the firm did for him, he couldn't answer anything I was asking him especially after I read the Evidentiary Hearing transcripts, so I told him, never to ask me to help him again, because I will not, and I didn't. I went directly on to the next client. My work was real. I didn't have any time for games, and not being taken seriously. I loved what I did with law and I was not about to take it for granted.

My next case, was with a guy by the name of Rashid, from Brooklyn, New York, but he got his case in Virginia. He had 27 years, and he had just come to Atlanta. He was a young guy, no more than 25 years of age. So we were talking in the unit one day after he had told us he was from the East Coast, and he was telling me about his case. It was a drug and gun case. He wanted me to look at the information he had on the case from Court. I told him I was not able to at the moment, because I was doing something else. So I didn't look at his case until I was finished researching and looking at some other things on something else with the firm. A few weeks later I took the case over with the firm. Rashid had six good issues we thought and one of them was his mental illness.

I judged Rashid based on his mental illness, because he appeared to be delusional to me. I asked him about what kind of gun it was; he told me a Mac 10. I then asked him why he did not appeal. He told me that his lawyer would not appeal, because he had waived all of his rights away by pleading out to the case. I then asked him about what kind of drugs he pleaded guilty to; he told me 500 grams of cocaine, not crack. I asked him several questions about his mental health; he told me some personal things about that. I went on and on, until I felt whether or not I would or would not be able to take the case and bring it to The Firm. Eventually, I did bring it to the firm and eventually we did win it for him and he went back to court, and we went on to our next case with a guy, nick named Drake. He was about 21 years old and had a life sentence for drugs. One day a friend of mine by the name of Cowboy introduced Drake to me and asked me could I look over his case. I told Cowboy let me see what he has. By looking at him I said to myself, dam this guy looks like a little kid, too young to be in here, especially in Atlanta USP. But there he was right there with us. A few days went by and I looked the case over. I told Cowboy and Drake together that yeah The Firm would take this one, so we took it. I started asking Drake a series of questions of course, and got down to business with the young fella. I honestly felt somewhat sorry to see him with a life sentence being so very young. I drew up a Title 28 U.S.C. Section 2255 motion for him. I cited the necessary cases concerning why he should have received an appeal. Roe v. Ortega, 528 U.S. 470 (2000). I cited ineffectiveness in counsel, prejudicing the petitioner by not filing an appeal upon the petitioner's request to do so. I stated that Drake had a Sixth Amendment right under the United States Constitution to a direct appeal upon request to counsel on the day of sentencing, and that counsel should have filed an appeal upon the petitioner's request to do so. I cited Roe v. Ortega, 528 U.S. 470 (2000). I stated that counsel had not only prejudiced the Petitioner, but that counsel had denied the petitioner due process to his Sixth Amendment rights to a direct appeal by not filing it. I cited Gomez Diaz v. United States, 433 F.3d 788-793 (11th Cir. 2005). I asked the Court who in their right mind would not want to appeal a life sentence? As I would go on and on doing these cases, I came to eventually realize that it was an African American thing that these Judges were putting away mostly African Americans for drugs for long periods of time. They were committing genocide of my people by locking them down for multiple years of their lives for little or no drugs and a lot of them for hardly any drugs at all. Most of the time, the drugs were the weight of a nickel or less than the amount that would fit into a coffee cup. My brothers were receiving 15 years to life, and even multiple life sentences for these drug crimes. It was the African American politicians in the Congress, the black caucus, and the churches, as well as the African American communities that had pushed for these laws to be enacted, in both the state and Federal arenas. No one, not even African Americans, want to see their neighborhoods flooded with crack, heroin, and other types of drugs, so they had pushed their legislators to pass and enforce these laws in both state and Federal. That was the reason why so many African Americans were being incarcerated. They knew ahead of time that these laws would put young African Americans away for long periods of their lives in Federal and state prisons. As time went on, the European Judges began to use it as a weapon of racism, and isolate African Americans for even longer periods of time because the African American politicians had already paved the way for them to do that by pushing for harsher laws against their own. Now, excessive time and multiple life terms is the result of this. The President knows all of this already, he's trying to do the best he can with what he can concerning this issue. Now, is he doing enough? Personally, I would say he's trying hard enough. I saw why Drake got the life sentence for such a very small amount of crack cocaine, and intended to argue his case accordingly and I did.

I explained to the Court in South Carolina, that Drake's Mother had been on drugs and in and out of drug treatment programs. Drake had, most of the time since he was a little kid of nine years of age, been left with his sister and two younger brothers to fend for themselves along with his Grandmother, who was very old and could only do so much for them, but was always there for them. I said Drake had been around drugs all of his life and that he hardly went to school, because at times he had been out looking for his Mother and hoping that nothing had happened to her so he couldn't go to school. I explained how Drake even had to steal at times so his two little brothers and sister could eat. I went deep. I told the judge, there's no young, 19-21 year old whites in Atlanta USP with life terms for the amount of drugs the weight of a nickel or the amount that could hardly fit into a coffee cup. I finished the case and I told him to sign several places, and that one goes to the court and one goes to the U.S. Attorney's Office in the District of South Carolina, Charleston Division. I waited a few months and received a response from the government, which I responded back. I remember Drake telling me that the Judge was a very hard and racist type of Judge. I would find out when the Court sent the order back that he had no racism in him from what I read in the order. He was a very nice Judge and a very respectful Judge at that. He called Drake in and gave him an Evidentiary Hearing, then after the hearing gave Drake 19 years and took the life back. When I heard the news I felt happy for the young fella and I thought back to myself and all the time I still had- 5 life terms plus 135 years. I was still fighting. I just got stronger and more into the law every chance I got. Drake had been my first life sentence I had ever won. I would go on to win another life sentence for another guy in the future.

I went on with the firm taking more cases and

winning them, but I was beginning to see that I could get myself "free" and that I was able to win. God gave me a gift in law, because it wasn't something I just liked, it was something I loved doing all day every day. I love it. I ate it. I slept with it. I did everything with the idea of always thinking law. It was me all the way. I wanted to do nothing else, with the exception of working out two hours a day. No matter where I was, it was about the law. I spoke it, I slept it, I wanted it, and I couldn't live without my "law and law books".

I didn't see "time" anymore, I couldn't, I had to learn to pretend that it simply didn't exist anymore or that I could live forever, because I was serving 5 life terms, plus a Ball 135. There was no way I could live that long. So I pretended it didn't exist. I had to, in order to live, in order to survive, and in order to stay focused on my Freedom. I still could not see through the tunnel, because I wouldn't know where I was going. So I stayed focused for the light to one day lead me out of the tunnel and into total light. It was on a Sunday morning and I'll never ever forget it. While in Atlanta in A-3 unit, there was an African American officer, dark complexion, about five nine, 190 pounds, glasses, who was a real cool guy. I was coming out of my cell to try to catch CNN news in one of the t.v. rooms. As I was walking past the officer, he said, "No law books today young man." No law library. It is not open today. They stopped letting us go on Sunday mornings. He told me to keep up the good work and that one day I'll get out of there. He asked me, how much time I had. I told him that I had 5 life terms, plus 135 years, with life for both the state and the FEDS. He told me to just keep trying, because he's seen guys like me before. I asked him what he meant by that? He said he used to work at a state prison with death row inmates. He used to take them off death row back and forth to court. Suddenly, I got very interested in everything he was saying to me. It was as if he and I were the only ones in the entire world at that time. I started asking him all kinds of questions about whether or not those guys stayed up day and night studying their cases? He said not all of them did, but those that do, they help their lawyers to help themselves. They study their cases, and help the lawyers see things that they might miss or don't see. He said those are the ones that usually end up getting off death row. He also said that they had death row inmates that just do nothing and let the lawyers do all the work. They are the ones that end up dying on death row. He told me a lot of very interesting and positive things that encouraged me to be where I am now in the thinking process of the law. From that day on, I never ever stopped talking to that correctional officer. Every time I saw him, no matter where I was, I made sure I either said hello or asked him a series of questions about what he remembered about those jail house death row lawyers in Georgia on death row. One thing he always said though, was for me to keep trying and to never ever give up. I must admit, I felt so much respect for the guy about how he would look me in my eyes as if he knew that if I kept going in the direction I did that I would one day be successful. In other words, he knew how to say things to me in a way that encouraged me to stay focused. And that I did.

There was another officer and, we'll call him Bout-it-Bout-it. He was real cool too. I confess I had never met officers like these two guys. They were street guys, who were very intelligent, and they acted as if they knew me and they were able to relate to me immediately and I to them. I really do not know how to explain it any other way. Anyway, Bout-it-Bout-it was so cool. We used to converse about Atlanta, the streets of Atlanta, Stone Mountain, and a lot of things. He was simply a cool officer. I can't say it any other way. He hated rats, and snitches. He had already checked me out, my background, and everything. Bout-it-Bout-it was the truth, and nothing but the truth. We laughed and talked all the time. He loved Chicken Man from Chicago. He always was very happy to see Chicken Man, because Chicken Man was always saying crazy funny ass jokes that evoked laughter. Bout-it-Bout-it just loved Chicken Man being around. Bout-it-Bout-it would always ask Stone where Chicken Man was, and I would go get Chicken Man for him and the three of us wouldn't stop laughing for hours. Bout-it-Bout-it was nothing but the truth. I'll always wish him and the other officer the best. I learned valuable things from them both and may God bless them always.

After years at Atlanta, I left via a transfer, to Coleman F.C.I. Medium, in Coleman, Florida. My Case Manager, a Mr. Wagner, informed me that when I stay out of trouble and walk a straight line, it wouldn't be hard to get to where I want to go. I thanked him for the transfer and let him know that it's greatly appreciated. I had learned from being in the penitentiaries for over 10 years, that I never wanted to see another penitentiary ever again, because I knew by getting stuck in them, I would never be able to work on my case as diligently as I needed to in order to one day see "FREEDOM". I also knew that I had better continue to walk a straight line, stay out of unnecessary conflict or I would be right back behind the wall, and handicapped from doing a lot of law work. I didn't need that and I wasn't playing myself back to the pen for nobody nor nothing unless it was unavoidable- unless one of my homeboys needed me desperately, because I couldn't violate the code. I had come too far, and there wasn't going to be no violating, if someone did then I would have to see the pen again. So one night, the officers came for me and told me I was going now on a transfer. They told me to leave my stuff there and that they would take care of it. Immediately, I thought back to myself about how I was transferred and traveled on that dam military helicopter. I wondered to myself, *"Did they forget that I was no longer on high security alert, or on that high security stuff?"* As I was leaving I gave D.C. Dog my watch, and I told him to keep my watch and to make sure I get all of my property. D.C. Dog did it with the utmost honesty and sincerity. Dog had been down for 22 years already and real he was to the death (family). I went down stairs and into the basement area with all the other inmates, from everywhere all over the world, not just this country, but all over the world. I waited with them for about four or five hours. We were chained up and put on a bus; which, I was happy to be on a bus, so I would be able to see things. We rode on to Coleman F.C.I. Medium, in Coleman, Florida. I was happy for the privilege and opportunity to be able to go from F.C.I. to F.C.I. Remember, my name was Sly Green, according to the media, the press, and the witnesses, a very so-called dangerous guy, a crime boss, a leader, a Godfather, and a cold blooded notorious gangster from Buffalo, New York. This is what was always being written about me. To me and those that knew me well, I was just Donald, a normal person like anyone else, who had just taken a fall. There were many Sly Greens in the FEDS from all over the world, and they too were the perfect gentlemen. The press, the media and newspapers had blown that name Sly Green up so big on the East Coast that I would never get out of prison if you believed anything they were saying and/or printing in those newspapers. But, I was glad not to be in high security anymore, Yes, I thanked God for all that too.

CHAPTER SEVEN

LEAVING ALL THE PENITENTIARIES FINALLY AND ENTERING INTO A TOTALLY DIFFERENT PRISON ENVIRONMENT

After going through the penitentiaries, I had learned to be very careful about myself, my existence, my speech, my personality, my way of thinking, and how I conducted myself period. In other words I had become penitentiary wise and intelligent as to how to stay alive while being in Federal penitentiaries and possibly having to do the rest of my natural life in them. I got the feel, I now knew my way through, and how to move through it all. But it is and was completely different once I entered into the Federal Correctional Institution, also known as an F.C.I. Those guys, the mass majority of them, didn't have a mother's clue as to how those Federal Penitentiaries functioned. They had only heard some things about them. There was so much disrespect in the F.C.I.'s among prisoners with each other, that I could not believe it. I would usually stop and ask myself, will I make it through because I was dealing with some damn retards in those F.C.I.'s. Those guys had no respect, not just for themselves, but not even for each other. I realized immediately that I was in an environment of mostly misfits and tarts. I also saw some guys from the pens. Most of them were basically the same, but some as usual fell into the F.C.I. mode. I would realize later on, that it was the only way you could stay there, because if you keep it penitentiary, you would not last. Those F.C.I. guys, would find a way to get you out of there on a transfer, because of the fear you

58

instilled. The manner in which you carried yourself, those F.C.I. guys simply were not used to it, and many of them didn't have a Mother's clue what they would be up against concerning what I had just gone through for over 10 years in those pens. So I too, had to change some things about myself. I had to become more liberal, more compassionate and understanding, and I had to look the other way about other things and I had to smile a lot more and don't be so very serious all the time and direct. I had to readjust would be a better word for it all. Believe me, I did. Because I never ever wanted to see those penitentiaries ever again. I needed more hours in the law library. And less lock downs, and a lot of other things as well. I had seen the light, but now I had to get through the tunnel that was blocking completely all of my FREEDOM. There was no light in that tunnel, so I had to create some through all of that darkness so I could one day see some FREEDOM. I stayed on top of the Firm. Big King was no more, because he was left at Bennettsville, South Carolina. I would hear from him every now and then through messages and letters. He was still "Firm," and I had taken on the task of building them everywhere I went- always with Big King's name and respect in the forefront, because it is he who had created it, and I intended to let those who joined our Firm know about Big Darnell King. I went on firming and then one day in May 2011, it happened. I went to a New York State parole board on the 25 year to life sentence. They asked me a question I never suspected they would. They (parole board) asked me, "How long have you been in Federal custody?" I said for over 20 years. They said we didn't know that Mr. Green. I was baffled by the response in a very curious way. They told me to come back next month and I did. When I appeared, I was told again come back in a few more months, and I did. They asked me about the murders, and my younger brother. I told them that I had not committed any murder at all, and that witnesses by the names of Steven Brown and Mr. James Wright, had fabricated a lie against me. Mr. Brown was from Brooklyn, New York, and at the time in Buffalo, New York was facing some charges of his own and lied to a jury about what he must have read in newspapers and testified against me based on newspaper articles. And then there was a James Wright, who testified against me, and created a story from the state prosecutor's office in Erie County from District Attorney Mr. Frank Clark, and Joseph Mursack. Mr. Wright was paid over $250,000.00 dollars for his lies and a personal check for $25,000.00 dollars from Mr. Frank Clark, the Assistant District Attorney at that time. They actually paid Mr. Wright for his testimony, and dropped Steven Brown's charges that he had been facing, just to convict me. The parole board told me that they had known about all of this, but that was not what they were there for. The next time I saw them they said they think it's time for me to start serving my Federal sentence now of four life terms, plus 110 years. I'll always believe they said it because of Mr. Davis, my Coleman F.C.I. Counselor, and Mr. Gage, my Case Manager. I believe they told the New Nork State parole board about how I was helping a lot of the inmates with their legal work, and that I was not a problem inmate. I believe they said very positive things to the New York parole board on my behalf and that was why I was released from New York state custody on to New York State parole. I'll never forget May 11th, 2011. It was surely one of the happiest days in my life when Mr. Gage said, "Mr. Green, I have something for you." I was in the cell looking for something and as I turned around I realized it was my Case Manager, Mr. Gage and I stopped in my tracks to see what he was saying. He said, "Mr. Green, I've got some good news for you." But of course I didn't know what he wanted and he handed me the papers and I looked – they said I was paroled from the State of New York on May 11th, 2011. I immediately saw some light in the tunnel. I hugged Mr. Gage on impulse. "Mr. Green, you can't hug me!" Man, but I didn't realize that I had. I was so happy. After I realized that, damn! I know I can win on the Federal joint. I started studying twice as much as I usually did. I went straight crazy into Federal law learning any and everything I could for a win on my case, and I've managed to stay that way, because now I can see some light. All I have to do is stay focused. I'll always be very grateful to Mr. Davis and Mr. Gage, for allowing me to see some light. My whole life changed at that moment. I came back into focus, I woke completely up. I saw FREEDOM, and refused not to allow anything to stop me from being Free. I know that the law library is my only way. I know that I'll die in here if I ever stop researching and studying and not staying focused. I know there is no parole or clemency for me- nothing but constant research and finding the key to my FREEDOM. Remember this! I have to know what I'm talking about because I have life without parole 4 times over, plus a Ball ten (110). I will never ever see the light of day in FREEDOM unless I win in court. The FEDS don't have parole. My only way to FREEDOM is through the law library. There is no other way out of here for me. I refuse to go any other way.

Because I would never ever sacrifice you nor anyone else to be Free, I live it for real, and if I die, in here, it will never ever be said or can ever be said that I did not try with all my heart and soul and mental facilities to win my FREEDOM. So if I go, let it be with Sly Green, fighting to the death with a pen in one hand and a legal pad in the other hand.

CHAPTER EIGHT

COLEMAN FEDERAL COMPLEX
COLEMAN FLORIDA

I arrived at Coleman in January of 2008, from Atlanta USP. The roaches, rats, snitches, cells, and the food was all terrible. I was tired of Atlanta and the filthiness of the place in general. But it had some very good things about it as well. One of them was the law library and the recreation and some very street wise and cool correctional officers.

After I got to Coleman, the officers took me immediately to the Special Housing Unit. I asked the Counselor lady Ms. Harris, who interviewed me, why she was sending me to lockdown. She said, "Mr. Sly Green, you are not coming into my population without first having a Captain's review. You were running a criminal enterprise on the streets."

I said, "A what?"

"A criminal enterprise Mr. Green. You were a Kingpin, and you are not coming out until you see a Captain."

I didn't see a Captain until a week later along with an Assistant Warden and another LT. All three of them interviewed me. They called me out of my cell into an office, and said they don't want any trouble here, and that if I was looking for some, they have some guys that will give it to me. They instructed me to do my time and go home. "Mr. Green, you've been doing very well, we see."

"I said YES! Sir! You'll have no problems out of me." I was released that day in the afternoon. When I touched the compound, it was big, beautiful and wide open. I couldn't believe I had made it this far from the roughest United States Penitentiaries to a sweet, beautiful spot like Coleman, F.C.I. I had finally made it to a spot that I would never ever want to leave unless I was going to a lower security prison, or straight home. Coleman was a dream come true. Immediately when I touched the compound, I saw guys from every prison I had ever been in. They paid their respects and I in turn paid mine back with respect and courtesy. I saw a friend of mine from Schyulkill, Pennsylvania, by the name of Yaw-Yaw. He was from the East Coast- Harlem, New York to be exact. He had heard I was there in the Special Housing Unit and was waiting for me to come out. He came to the law library and brought one of my Buffalo, New York homeboys with him by the name of Cyrus Benning. Cyrus, Yaw-Yaw, and I would forever be together after that along with Inch, from Rochester, New York. We were all very close. We hung close almost every day. They would come to the law library. This law library had computers. No more books, everything was on computers now. So I had to learn how to work those computers, and that I did. Cyrus would pull up things for me, and show me how to work it. He was a genius on the computers. After about six hours a day in the law library, I would go out for an hour or two and work out because in order to stay focused, you have to keep your body and mind in shape and so I never forgot that Big King had always told me don't stay in that law library all day all the time. He would say, "Go out and free your mind, stay on your workouts too." So I never forgot that and sometimes I would still stay in that law library doing legal work all day, because I would forget about time, and I would be in a totally different world in law. It was a world I loved living in. I was doing cases, researching, talking to the guys about cases. I would forget that I had time limits. I would even forget to go on certain call-outs. I just loved what I did, plain and simple and nothing else really mattered.

After being in Coleman and on the compound for a few days, word got out that (Stone) Sly Green from the East Coast was there and that I was a giant in the law- that I was a genius in it, that I was a professor in it, and that convicts spoke about some of the cases they had heard I had won. Like I said before, there were guys there from every joint I had ever been in. They all, I must admit, spoke very highly of me, more so than I would have ever expected. But was I a giant now. Was I as good as they said I was? You be the judge of that.

When I got to Coleman, I had already won approximately 52 cases or more. It would be at Coleman that I would truly find out who I really was in the legal world. Coleman would be the joint to put me over the top, and make me Federal famous in the law, because it would be at Coleman that I would win more cases than I had in any other joint. It would be at Coleman that I would win two life sentences, making it a total of three altogether. It would be at Coleman that I got to spend crazy time in the law library, because I had a job in the chapel directly connected to the law library. It would be at Coleman that I would win some of my best cases ever. Coleman would be a total of 133 wins for the "FIRM-" the Firm Big King had put together 12 years ago in Schyulkill, Pennsylvania. The same Firm that Big King and the others who had joined us would put together in other joints when they transferred. Coleman made me what I became and that was the best that I could be.

After a few months and getting to know the guys, I started interviewing guys for researchers, and typists.

Cyrus would become a researcher as well as pull up whatever I needed. I took Cyrus for a researcher on the computer because he knew a little legal work and especially how to operate the computer. I took a white guy for the typist, we'll call him Slim. I was the only jail house lawyer on the Firm. I gave them the Firm's history and we went to work from there. As time went on I got two more researchers, two more typists and two other jail house lawyers within the next two years of being in Coleman. I took the joint completely over and the Firm dominated it. Now, case after case! I remember my first case at Coleman. It was about crack cocaine. We will call him Billy Boy, because that was his nick name, and he was from St. Petersburg, Florida. I did a Title 18 U.S.C. Section 3582(c)(2) Motion for Billy Boy about the crack law U.S.S. GUIDELINE Amendment 706.

The Section 3582(c)(2) I filed for Billy Boy, came back from the Judge about 30 days later, and the Judge in the Middle District of Florida, Tampa Division, asked Billy Boy to send him a reason as to why he (the Judge) should depart further down under Title 18 U.S.C. Section 3553(a), because Billy Boy was requesting even more time off then the two points under U.S.S. Guideline Amendment 706. I told Billy Boy to send in all of his educational and vocational achievements. But Billy Boy went behind my back without me knowing it, and had another jail house pro-se litigant file to the courts that he should receive another downward departure, because he had cooperated with the government and blew St. Petersburg up off the map on the snitching side.

This is what the response motion back to the court stated when the other jail house pro-se litigant showed it to me. He probably thought that Billy Boy had already told me, but he had not and had I known I would have never filed the motion at all. I would have checked Billy Boy and told him to never come at me like that ever again. He had to have known I was thinking something like that because he went behind my back and had someone do it for him. I told the other jail house pro-se litigant, "Hey, I don't know nothing about this. I don't want to have anything to do with this period. Leave me out of this." After that incident with Billy Boy, I double checked the cases I reviewed before I took them and straight out asked them is there anything else I should know. But, every so often, I must confess, that I would hear things about certain clients, but it was never in their paperwork when I checked it thoroughly and thereafter, if it was not correct information from a reliable source, I would inform the Firm to pursue the case until or unless we had solid information that that particular client was a rat or snitch or had cooperated with the government or on his case or whatever case. I simply needed the evidence to be exactly sure.

Billy Boy I left alone, and any others like him that I had solid proof on. My next case was with a guy we'll call Lindsey. He too was from Florida, the Southern District of Florida. They called it the "Muk", I guess because of the mud in Belle Glade, Florida. I was roommates along with another guy in the cell with Lindsey. I was on the stool, looking at the wall, because I had just come into B-2 unit and I was told I was going to 71 cell. It had three beds on top of each other. It was my first time seeing that in the FEDS, in all the 15 years I had already been incarcerated. Anyway, Lindsey asked me was I a Chico (Puerto Rican), and I said, "No, I'm African American, and proud of it." He then told me again that I look like a Chico. I said again, "But I'm not. I'm black and proud of it and I don't have any

Chico in me.   I'm all black, but it's nothing wrong with being a Chico anyway. So why are you asking me that?"

He said, "Oh it's nothing man!" Then he asked me how long have I had been down.   I told him 15 years, and he said I don't look like it. I was thinking to myself what the hell am I supposed to look like? Then he ask me where I was from. I told him, the East Coast, Buffalo, New York. He spoke of Rochester, New York, and I told him it was only 45 minutes away from Buffalo. He then went on to ask me what I do, and I said I do legal work. Suddenly he jumped out of his bed from the top near the ceiling and before he could pull his legal work out of his locker, the other guy under him pulled his stuff from under his mattress and asked me if I will look at this for him.

By that time Lindsey was pulling his paper work out, saying "Yo! Man! I dreamed you were coming, I prayed for you to come, I read my Bible every day. I prayed for you. Here. Please look at mine after you look at Markay's, please man, Yo! What's your name, man! Mine is Bud Lindsey, Yo! Please Man! I prayed for you to come, I asked God to send you to me, please help me man!"

I was not amazed or anything. I was just flabbergasted. I just could not believe what I was hearing. Well, I looked at Markay's work, and I supplemented to it a few weeks later. I then looked at Lindsey's work for over eight months and I kept wondering why all the other guys were going to two man rooms and not me. Well, Lindsey had told the Case Manager to leave me in the cell with him, because I was helping him on his case. I did not know he was doing that though until over 13 months later, after I had done his case and supplemented to it for him and I couldn't get rid of him, so one day I asked my Counselor when was I going to a two man room and Mr. Davis, a very nice Counselor, told me that I could have been sent to one before now. I knew then that Lindsey had kept me in that cell all that time without knowing it. We submitted the Section 2255 motion, which was about nine issues. Lindsey had an armed career offender status case, with possession of a weapon (a firearm). He had gotten 25 years for it because he had been classified an armed career offender. I attacked his armed career offender status. I attacked his arrest based on an illegal search and seizure of the car and how they apprehended the firearm. I attacked the three state priors they used to arm career him. I used Shepard v. United States, 544 U.S. 13, 26 (2005). And Taylor v. United States, 495 U.S. 575 (1990), had been violated based on required Shepard documentation in regards to the state priors. I also argued that the proper requirements of the modified categorical approach had not been used to arm career Lindsey. I stated how in United States v. Day, 465 F.3d 1265 (11th Cir. 2006), how Lindsey had pled to one thing in the state priors, but his presentence report had him pleading to the original arresting charges, when in fact, he had not. I stated that a presentence report is not evidence, and that petitioner had in fact, objected to his presentence report at his sentencing hearing and to his counsel. I stated that one of the state priors was a misdemeanor offense, not a felony and that therefore, it could not be used to have enhanced him to career offender status. I attacked another state prior that he had for a gun possession and that according to Begay v. United States, 128 S.Ct. 1581 (2008); United States v. Archer, 531 F.3d 1347 (11th Cir. 2008). And Johnson v. United States, 130 S.Ct. 1265 (2010), that the gun charge could not now be used to arm career him because possession of a weapon was not a violent offense according to <u>Begay</u>, <u>Archer</u>, and <u>Johnson</u>. I attacked the illegal search in violation of his Fourth Amendment rights under the United States Constitution. A few months later the government responded with a request for a sixty day extension. I was happy of course, because it gave me a longer time to stay on top of the case and keep my wits sharp in the law. The next time the government responded they sent 83 pages altogether with a request to the court for the additional pages to be accepted. I was cool with it because it's what I loved doing. Legal work. I went to work, day and night, night and day until I finished the response. After I finished it, I never knew Lindsey was taking my work to other jail house pro-se litigants to look over, that had never been to any penitentiaries, doing law; were on the streets for 10 years before they even came to Federal prison and I had been in 15 years already. They didn't know what they were talking about, they hadn't been tested. They hadn't been in even long enough to even know what to do with law books. Yet he was allowing them to advise him, put this in, take this out. It just so happened that I accidently caught on to him one day when this damn fool didn't want to pursue his <u>Begay</u> and <u>Archer</u> claim. So I said, "Lindsey, who you been talking to, to tell you something so dumb and illiterate as not to pursue your <u>Begay</u> and <u>Archer</u> claim?" I was feed up with the guy being so dumb and unintelligent, that I said, Lindsey, how is it that you can be here with me for over 18 months now, and in 10 minutes, a bunch of damn fools can change your mind about your legal work, and now you suddenly don't want your <u>Begay</u> and <u>Archer</u> claims in your 2255 motion responses, because your Homeboys told you they don't apply?

"You can't predict the future," Lindsey stated.

I said, "What does that have to do with anything, Lindsey?" I said, "Man! That's crazy!" But I didn't realize that Lindsey was straight illiterate, uneducated and could barely read and write. Anybody could mislead him and ill advise him and he would go for anything that sounded good to him, whether fiction or illusions, so he would go for anything. Once I realized that about him, I said, "Lindsey, if you don't go all the way with this <u>Begay</u> and <u>Archer</u> claim, and with all of my claims I submitted and allow me to continue to respond to them all until I win this case, whether on the District Court level or Appeal level, then I'm off the case." Because Harvey and all his homeboys were selling him all kinds of illiterate dreams of which they had absolutely no idea what they were saying. I said, "Damn, Man! Harvey is a typist, not a pro-se litigant." After I went through all of this he ended up winning in the Eleventh Circuit and walked right out the front gate a freeman. He never said Thank You. He never reached back, he never did any of the things a gentlemen of appreciation would do. He was cold & lame, and that's word up! His stupidity and illiteracy almost kept him in a Federal U.S. prison for 25 years.

My next case was one that the whole firm took on together, and we'll call him Simple. He was a Jamaican guy and had been incarcerated for over 20 years. Simple had a life sentence for drugs- crack cocaine to be exact. I filed a Title 18 U.S.C. Section 3582(c)(2) for Simple. It was based on the U.S.S. Guideline Amendment 706. The 706 Amendment lowered Simple's base offense level plus he had a 505 Amendment that was good for him too, but could not be used until the 706 Amendment surfaced, because he still would have

had too many points and that would have still left him
with a life sentence.   What I did was put the 505 and
the 706 Amendments together in his Section 3582(c)(2)
motion and got six points lowered rather than just two
and that left the Judge the discretion to either release
him or hold him for 13 more months. The Judge gave
him 25 years, as he already had over 20 years in, so he
had good time coming too, and I was happy for him.
Then he started talking about he should get more time
off than the Judge gave him, and I told him he should be
grateful for the Judge taking the life off of him, as he
now only had 13 months left and he can go back to
Jamaica and live the rest of his life. The next day I saw
him he started talking about he was an Egyptian Pharaoh
in another life. I said, "Simple, I'm through with you
(family)," and I never spoke to him ever again after that.
He left about two weeks later after the Judge sent him a
new sentencing order with a change of sentence. The
Title 28 U.S.C. Section 2241(c)(3) I had filed for him was
no longer needed, so I never mentioned it to him during
our discussions. I really didn't know what to make of
him after he came at me with the Pharaoh joint.
Bloodhound from Miami, Florida, told him too, that he
was a very lucky man to have that life off of him, but he
didn't see anything me or Bloodhound was saying to him
after the Pharaoh business. The Firm had done Simple
well and was prospering in Coleman, but everyone
couldn't understand the sudden change in Simple.

The next case was a guy that we'll call John-John,
from Miami, Florida. I took the case myself with some
assistance every now and then from the Firm. John-
John's case was a Hobbs Act case and a weapons case. A
Title 18 U.S.C. Section 924(e) case. John-John had
already been incarcerated for over 17 years. I filed a Title

28 U.S.C. Section 2241(c)(3) motion for him, based on his actual, factual, and legal innocence. I fought John-John's case for over 3 years. I blew it in the Middle District of Florida on jurisdiction and had to appeal it to the Eleventh Circuit Court of Appeals. John-John paid the $505.00 dollar filing fee and we filed a pro-se Appellant Brief. We were given a stay based on Bryant v. Warden, No.: 12-11212; Mackey v. Warden, No.: 12-14727; and McKinney v. Warden, No.: 12-12953-CC. All Eleventh Circuit cases, based on jurisdiction of actual, factual, and legal innocence in regards to the "savings clause" of Title 28 U.S.C. Section 2255(e), by entry of a Title 28 U.S.C. Section 2241(c)(3) motion. We used Bryant, Mackey, McKinney, Descamps v. United States, 133 S.Ct. 2275 (2013; Begay v. United States, 128 S.Ct. 1581 (2008); and Johnson v. United States, 130 S.Ct. 1265 (2010). We stated that the State of Florida priors used to enhance John-John to armed career offender status were invalid, inadequate, and insufficient to test the legality of his detention. We stated that John-John's armed career offender status was improper, unconstitutional and a manifest injustice, because the Judge used the presentence report to enhance John-John over his own objections to it, and that the presentence report was not a legally certified document that could be used to enhance the Appellant over his objections. A presentence report was not evidence, especially when you object to it. The information in it, as John-John objected thereto, then the government cited other state priors that it had not cited over 15 years ago. I cited Canty v. United States, 570 F.3d 1251 (11th Cir. 2009), and explained to the Appeals Court as I had already done with the lower court that the government cannot now come with new state priors 15 years later, when it

had the opportunity to do so 15 years ago. I said the government like the defendant is only allowed one opportunity and no more to present the priors it's going to use. I put Canty down. I also, stated that according to Shepard v.United States, 544 U.S. 13, 26 (2005); and Taylor v. United States, 496 U.S. 575 (1990), that improper documentation was used to armed career the appellant, that it was not certified legal documentation as required by Shepard, nor was modified categorical approach used either. I stated that it could not have been, because John-John's State of Florida priors were all in the early 80's, and also, that when he was on Federal trial for his Federal case, all of his state priors had already been destroyed, so there could never have been a modified categorical approach on his state priors to verify Descamps required element approach, divisible or indivisible. Because Shepard nor Taylor, didn't even exist. I stated that there was nothing to compare the state priors with. Because no state prior documentation existed for any comparison or anything period. I gave this case like all the rest, all I had and all I was worth. I wanted nothing more than to win.

As I wrote the appeal brief for John-John, I flashed back to Tampa Mase, a giant in the pro-litigant world in the Federal System. I wondered how Mase would see this case. I said when I finish, I'm taking it over to B-3, for the professor Mase to see it. Because maybe I might be forgetting something and Mase will surely find it if I am. I flashed back to all of the years I had seen law for over 20 years straight, damn near every single day. I loved it so much, I just couldn't give it a rest unless I got those migraine headaches, then I'd have to stop for a week or so, because that's how long they would last sometimes. I flashed back to Meeka, and

Walker, the Lewisburg crew, and to Mr. Gibson. I thought about what would they do with this case. I thought about Leon, the one who had forced my hand in learning how to write the law, I flashed deeper back to Tommy Rutledge, Rusty, and Mr. Skinner, Chicago Shaw and Robb. I said to myself, how would they look at this case. I wanted nothing more than to win it all the way, because I knew that this was a Section 2241(c)(3) motion, based on actual, factual, and legal innocence. I felt I had convinced the Appeals Court that John-John was actually, factually and legally innocent of his armed career offender status, based on Bailey v. United States, 516 U.S. 137 (1995); Bousley v. United States, 523 U.S. 614-620 (1998); Davis v. United States, 417 U.S. 333-346 (1974); Engle v. Isasc, 456 U.S. 107-126; Hill v. United States, 417 U.S. 333-346 (1974); Engle v. Isasc, 456 U.S. 107-126; Hill v. United States, 368 U.S. 424-429 (1962); Schlup v. Delo, 513 U.S. 298 (1995); Fiore v. White, 531 U.S. 225-228 (2001); Begay, Johnson, and Descamps, supras.

I had put the case to the firm for an opinion of what it thought. I flashed back to Mr. Turkcores, and thought to myself, what he and Mr. Daniels would say about this brief. I thought and thought, and I went over and over it until I felt a win coming. Then I flashed back once more into the past and thought how the other jail house pro-se litigants with the exception of Cornhead and Mase, had said don't pay the filing fee, wait for some other case to come out and try that. Because I'll lose if I pay the filing fee of $505 dollars. I had looked at John-John and him if he doesn't pay him, I'm going all the way with it, without him. I'm not blowing this joint for nobody. I saw the win, I felt it and I wanted it to happen and nothing was going to stop me from going all the way with this joint. Mackey, McKinney, and Bryant came down on the 24th of December, 2013, I had this case for over 3½ years in Court, now I had a stay and then when Mackey, McKinney, and Bryant won, and I had the stay, 30 days later the Appeals Court said brief it. I had gone extremely too much with the case partially with the Firm, to just let it slip away like that. John-John had paid the filing fee, I was very happy about him believing in me, and my work. I stayed up for days on the Appeal. I filed it when the required 30 days and after the government had sent me their response, I smashed them, or least I feel I did, because the appeals court hasn't said anything to me yet. So I went on to my next case, still waiting on the John-John decision. My next case was a Mexican guy, he was very young when he was arrested by the FEDS. He had two car jackings and had blown trial and all of his appeals. We'll call him Mexico.

One day I came back from the law library at about 8:30 in the evening, and there was this very young Mexican kid standing at my door. I said, "What's up Mexico? How can I help you?" He said he was wondering if I could help him because he just blew all of his appeals on direct. I said, "I'm busy right now, but let me see what I can do for you or if there is anything I can do for you." He went immediately to his cell and got his legal work and brought it to me. I told him to get with me in about two weeks and I'll let him know if I can do anything for him, based on what I have the researchers read and check into on what he just gave me. But I took it myself and read over it and asked As-Sadiq if he would check it out along with young Magnum that were both on The Firm. Both taught the Law classes to the inmate population of approximately 1700 inmates, with not even 50 of them ever filled up any of our legal classes.

After we all looked over the young Florida Mexican's paper work, I did six issues for him, especially on his mental illness, and the stacking of his sentencing counts. Because his counts were stacked on top of each other and unconstitutionally applied in the way that it was done, we attacked it. A case had just come down on it and we used that case too, as persuasive. Because it was from another circuit, the Sixth Circuit to be exact. We put the Florida v. Nixon, 125 S.CT.551 issue into it because he played absolutely no part in his defense at all. We went with the Atkins v. Virginia, 576 U.S. 304 (2002), case on the mental illness along with Title 18 U.S.C.SECTION 4241. After filing the Section 2255 Motion, the Court gave the Government two time extensions. Then a request came from the Mexican's lawyer to file an Affidavit against the young kid, stating that the information in his Section 2255 Motion was incorrect. The lawyer flipped on the Mexican and we had to battle with her, and two Assistant U.S. Attorneys, but a few months later the Judge ruled in our favor and gave the young Mexican, who was 22 years old, an Evidentiary Hearing on the issues that were presented. The young Mexican is still in a mental hospital, being evaluated. 38 years for such a young kid is extremely a lot of time. If he was not mentally ill, he definitely is now, with a 38 year sentence, and constantly stressing every day with all of that time to serve. He was already terribly stressed when I first met him. I honestly did not know if he was coming or going mentally. That was one of the Firm's main reasons for submitting a mentally ill issue along with the other issues.

Our next case was with a guy we'll call Bloodhound. He was from Miami, Florida. He was serving 3 life terms, for drug charges.   He had exhausted all of his appeals, and so I filed a Title 28 U.S.C. Section 2241(c)(3) Motion / Petition / Memorandum of Law. I went in on actual, factual, and legal innocence, based on a fundamental defect, and a manifest injustice, based on his being labeled a career offender on Florida State priors of the Florida State Statute of Section 893.13, which has no "mens rea" to the illicit nature of the substance to jury determination beyond a reasonable doubt. We hit them with Descamps v. United States, 133 S. Ct. 2275 (2013); Begay v. United States, for the other state prior that was supposedly a violent felony turned out under Begay; and the United States v. Johnson, 130 S.Ct 1265 (2010); not to be a violent offense and did not meet career offender requirements. Bloodhound's case has been pending now for at least 3 years, on that Section 2241(c)(3) Motion/ Petition/ Memorandum of Law.

Recently the Firm was looking at a case that Roy Black won on an appeal in the Eleventh Circuit for a guy that's here, and we'll call him Doc. He pled guilty and received up to 30 years even though he had won on appeal. He was afraid the FEDS were going to indict his whole family, so he was coerced into pleading guilty involuntarily, unintelligently, and unknowingly to 30 years on a plea agreement. I informed the doctor, that we would look over the case, and would get back to him after we decided who would be the point man on the case. I honestly believed though that Doc., did not have thirty years in him, because he looked tired and worn out and too exhausted, based on what I was seeing in him as we conversed about the case. Plus, I just couldn't see how his family could be indicted for something only he went to trial the first time for and they never indicted them then. We are considering the case as this book is being written. But from what we see thus far, there's no question we can get him back, because the plea was verbally coerced, under stress and duress, and extortion because the Doctor should not have been verbally forced into the plea involuntarily through threats of coercion. He never should have been told by the government nor counsel, that he cannot appeal such an involuntary plea. He has a Sixth Amendment right to under the United States Constitution.

If As-Sadiq wants to do it, it'll be a straight win, if not, he has his reasons for probably not wanting it.

As of right now, I have over 133 wins, and I mean wins not loses. There's no question about it. I have most of them by myself, along with the help from the Firm that Big Darnell King from Mount Vernon, New York (even though he loves to say he's from Harlem, New York) created. I'll always be very grateful to him, Big King, for what he created and for how we put Firms everywhere we went. I'll always remember how Big King used to say always let the client tell his "story." Because there's always a possibility we might be missing something or didn't know something. Big King always said, let the courts tell us yes or no! Not the inmates. Big King said a lot of things that made a lot of sense and came into use later on as we built our Firms everywhere we went. We teach law in classes, we can't walk down the compound without other inmates stopping us at least 30-40 times in a single day, and if something new comes out on a case, especially from the Supreme Court, it's been many times that many inmates stopping me, As-Sadiq, Young Magnum, and even our typist Slim, and the others.

Each morning that I awoke, the first thing on my mind is usually law, the last thing on my mind when I go to bed is unusually law. I love it; because I love myself, and the only way out of here for a guy that's been charged with Title 28 U.S.C. Section 848. 843, 846, 841(b)(1)(A), Title 1962-1963, is the law library. The only way out for a guy with a 73 count indictment with 32 codefendants, many of them never seen in my life before, is through the law library. I can't see any other way. And if I should decease lawyering for my Freedom as I have managed to do for the last 24 years of my life with a sentence of now four life terms, plus 110 years, because I'm no longer subjected to the state sentence. It's over. All I have is the Federal one. And I'm doing what I do, the best I can to win it. I'll never ever go crazy. I'll never ever complain about the sentence I have. I'll never ever blame anyone for my unfortunate situation. I don't feel sorry for myself, nor about myself. But if I had to do it all over again, I would go to law school and become a lawyer. It took coming here to bring the best of the best out of me. It took coming here for me to become who I've become. It took coming here for me to see that complaining won't do you any good if you're not trying to help yourself, because no one is going to hear you any way. I'm not upset, nor mad at anyone. If I never get my FREEDOM at least I died trying to. If I win my case and get FREEDOM, one day, I'll be very happy about that like anyone else would be after being incarcerated all of these years.

Coleman, Medium made me "me." I accomplished very little by myself in all these years without constant help from so many other jail house pro-se litigants. I became who I am in the law with most of my help and assistance from other jail house pro-se litigants like Mr. Skinner, Rusty Leon, Shawn, Tommy Walker, Meeka, Rick Turkeorse, and so many others, like

Slim the typist, too many to name. I've won as many times. Though the new inmates say behind my back, they haven't seen me win any cases, and that's because I don't win them every day. They (inmates) always have something to say whether it's good or bad. I remember one day I had a filling in my teeth. It was so bad, that I had to go to the hospital, but I went down and out of this world into a world I never knew existed. I was walking toward the light with an angel on my left side, telling me to keep walking toward this very indescribable beautiful light. People on both sides of me were screaming out loud, and the angel kept saying, just keep walking straight, don't pay them any attention and I did. Suddenly another angel came around from the other side as I was walking and said we are not ready for you yet, we still have a lot left for you to do. I said, "NO! Please! I want to come now," but the angel said, "No, we still have a lot left for you to do." The first angel had suddenly disappeared, and as I went to take another step, I couldn't because there was no bottom, no ending, and I stepped back. Suddenly I came back into this physical world and never again have I been as I used to be. I want nothing more than to win, win, and win. I feel I have a special gift for Law now, and that could be why I love it so much. I feel I was blessed with it from God. Sometimes when I do a case, it's like God is right there with me guiding my hand for a win. And I win it too. I'm at peace with myself. I don't worry about nothing. There's no reason to under my circumstances, because I know what it takes to get my "FREEDOM", that Law Library!

CHAPTER NINE

THE WORLD I LIVE IN - ONE

The world I live in has its own customs, language, style and ways. I truly understand how difficult it is for the public, a different class of people altogether, to understand how different convicts are from them. I know they (public) see us very differently and I truly respect the many different reasons why they see us the way they do. Because had I never been incarcerated, I would probably think and feel the same way the public feels about prisons. As a prisoner, I now also see the other side, the prisoner's side in regards to the Judges, Prosecutors, Wardens, U.S. Attorney's, and police agencies. They arrest and charge us with crimes. They usually lie and fabricate their cases against us 90% of the time. They no longer know what it is to be honest and truthful. They have become numb when it comes to honesty and truthfulness. For example, the Federal government will arrest your entire family just to get to you on a conspiracy charge knowing you had absolutely nothing to do with the crime your relatives may or may not have committed. The Federal system rules in fear, they extort a person into pleading guilty when arrested with the threat that if you go to trial we (Federal government) will put you away for as long as we can. They threaten you about going to trial, they punish you for going to trial and if you do proceed to trial they life you out, they give you all the time they can give you, just for exercising your Sixth Amendment right to a trial. The FEDS are vicious. They will lie on you and fabricate evidence against you. They will do anything to convict you, whether true or not. Their main purpose is to convict you by any means necessary. That is why 97% of the people charged with Federal crimes plead guilty. The other 3% go to trial and only one percent is acquitted and thereby, leaving the government a 99% conviction rate. The U.S. Attorneys, the Judges, and the police agencies, they all work together against you, whether you are innocent or not. 99% of the time, they are going to band together and convict you. There are very few Judges that will uphold the law on your behalf when it comes to crime and punishment, whether you are innocent or not. Now you know that justice in America is not blind, nor is it impartial or fair to people of color, especially African Americans in this country. But it is racist and ugly toward people of color, again, especially toward African Americans. Now you know that justice can see through the eyes of Europeans against people of color in America. They (European Judges) make sure you see it too. They (European Judges) put a face on justice, their face- especially when they sentence you. And remember this too, if you are a person of color, especially an African American, you can be actually, factually, and legally innocent and they (Judges) will not care, and convict and sentence you anyway. WHY? Because to them you are nothing but a minority or an African American without any rights.

I know what I'm saying is true. I've won 133 cases to this very day. I read cases all the time. I study law. I know law. I study lawyers and Judges, and U.S. Attorneys and prosecutors. What I see is what I'm writing. It is not something that I can just make up. All you see in these prisons are minorities and African Americans. Did they commit crimes? Of course a lot of them did, but some of them did not. 99% have a lot more time served than Europeans in these same prisons with them for less serious crimes than the Europeans. I know what it's like to go to trial on a state case. I know what it's like to go to trial on a Federal case. I know what it's like to be in a state prison, especially a high security one like Attica, New York, Auburn, New York, Green Haven, New York, Clinton, Dannamerora New York, and Shawangunk, New York. The highest of the highest maximum prisons in the State of New York. I was in all of them. I know what it's like in the Federal ones as well. I know the criminal justice system, both state and Federal are strongly biased towards people of color, especially African Americans. I know because I've experienced it myself, personally for 23 years and counting.

Enology, criminology, and the philosophy of the criminal justice system working on the prisoners through the wardens, and its administration, all the way from the Central Office in Washington, D.C. It's the system working against the prisoners. 99% of them being illiterate to the way, and working of the system don't understand what's going on right in front of them. Blind, deaf, and dumb to their very prison existence. Always complaining but never standing up for anything. Always complaining, but steadily murdering, assaulting, raping, snitching, and killing each other. Always complaining, but will not stand up for a better educational environment, better law library material to help them gain their Freedom, better living conditions, better food, etc... It's a damn shame. We will do everything negative against each other and get locked down for it for months and years at a time, but we won't volunteer to lock down for a year or two years, for something constructive and positive that will benefit us in society in the future when or if we are ever released. How do we expect anybody to help and assist us when all we do is self-destruct, and snitch on those who try to help and assist us. It's not the wardens, it's not Central Office. It's US. We are our own worse enemy and I write this Book to tell you exactly that. It's not easy describing these things to you and saying them to you. It pains me all the time to see what I see in these Federal United States prisons. Remember, these guys were gangsters on the streets, crime bosses, doctors, lawyers, murders, and killers, but yet in here they won't even stand up for better medical care. But they will hurt, crush, and disrespect each other, 24 -7. Now what does that tell you? How can you possibly help and or assist a group of people like these guys in the Federal system? We are locked in our cells for months and years for hurting each other, but we won't volunteer to lock in for better conditions, better law library materials, better education, better programs that the Central Office and the U.S. Senate took away over 20 years ago. What kind of people do not want to help themselves, knowing that one day they will be released back into society? Federal prisoners!!! We are treated like slaves in prison, because we accept it, and 99% of the time it's exactly how we allow ourselves to be treated unnecessarily. They treat their dogs and animals on the streets better than prisoners allow themselves to be treated.

It pains me dearly to have to write this, but somebody has to say it, for what it is! And it's our own fault. No one is responsible for how we allow ourselves to be treated but us. No one should ever be held responsible for the conduct that we exhibit toward each other, but ourselves. No one will ever be able to do anything about it, but us (prisoners). Because we are responsible for our own demise. When we do become responsible maybe then we will stand together without racism, without hurting, and assaulting, and killing and murdering and disrespecting each other. And say to each other, enough is enough. Let's all stand together as one for better education, better programs, better law library materials, better conditions, parole, goodtime, and respect for each other without hating and disrespecting each other. Somebody had to say it, and I chose to be that one.

CHAPTER TEN

THE WORLD I LIVE IN - TWO

The world I live in demands that I stay disciplined, in check and very persistent with my legal work in my quest to be FREE or I'll lose sight of where I am and what lies ahead of me. Because it's easy to do with all of these damn fools and the illiteracy in these damn prisons, especially the ones I've been exposed to. Therefore, I must stay logical and rational as much as possible. Despite the constant madness around me all the time.

My philosophy is totally different now, from what it once was. Now I choose only the legal way, the law way, and now I want nothing more than to be with my two sons and daughter, and help a lawyer win all the cases we can win together. Now I see the light, now I see my way, and because I have so much time to do and think, now I'm at peace with myself. I don't worry about anything at all. Because worrying won't do me any good. Plus, no one is going to hear me anyway. I did it to myself. I exposed myself to various influences, and manipulations based on various hustlers, and street manipulations as I was growing up in the environment from which I came. But, despite all of that, no one is to blame for anything in my past but me. I accept full responsibility for my past, present, and future. I've had an opportunity to look deep within myself, and ask myself a zillion questions, and I always come up with it's my own fault, my own obstacles, and hurdles, that I myself allowed to stop and prevent me from going the other way. I've got family members, and the Russells, who tried very hard to direct me in the right direction, but I was street poison. I loved the streets, more than I loved myself and FREEDOM. No one, is responsible for how my life has turned out, but me. I am and was 23 years ago, my own worst enemy. I did it all to myself. I put myself into these unfortunate positions and situations. Now look at me, I'm writing books about my change in life, about how much time I have and have already served. No matter what happens from here on out because now I see the light and guess what! It's never too late to change. I did!!! And I feel very positive about it too.

CHAPTER ELEVEN

THE WORLD I LIVE IN - THREE

I live in a world that despite all of the chaos, the controversies, altercations, murders, assaults, rapes, killings, and disrespect for each other, we as prisoners can one day band together in unity as one, and move this Federal prison system into a positive result of better education, college programs, better computers, better food, parole, reasonable good time credits, better living conditions and better communications with the Central Office, rather than being treated and looked as the scum of the earth. I'm asking all of my Federal prisoners in all of the Federal Institutions to communicate with each other positively. STOP the madness, STOP the jealousy, STOP the rating, snitching and informing on each other and bring non-violent unity among ourselves and stand up for a positive cause, rather than being confined in your cells for months and weeks at a time for the stupid things we always get confined for. And as for the shot callers, put your soldiers, your friends, and comrades together and stand up for something meaningful, something that we can all one day be proud of that we did altogether as one and let the American public see that we too, as prisoners can change for the better, for positive and constructive change. Rather than for disturbances and unnecessary riots and problems that we do not need. My fellow prisoners, I'm hurting because those of you just like me with 10, 20, 30, life and multi-life sentences, you don't seem to see the light, you don't seem to want your FREEDOM, and you don't want to stand up for a sentence change, based on the harshest drug laws in American history. You don't seem to see that you are incarcerated for ghost drugs, that you never had, that you were never ever arrested for. You don't seem to see what is happening to us with these Title 21 U.S.C.

Section 846, 848(a) and (b); Title 18 U.S.C. Section 1962-1963, narcotics conspiracy laws. You don't seem to see us all serving very harsh draconian and very severe sentences, for drugs the weight of a nickel, and those of us with life and multi-life terms for drugs that cannot even fit into a coffee cup. Yet here we are with foreigners serving much less time than ourselves for tons and multi-tons of drugs that they sent and brought to the shores of America, and they have little or no time to serve. Yet we get 10, 20, 30, life and multi-life terms for drugs the weight of a nickel and not even enough to fill a morning cup of coffee. My fellow prisoners, they lock us down for months and years in our cells for disciplinary reports that are usually miswritten and a lot of times made up of lies. They punish us for little or nothing, they take from us our privileges at will without repercussions. They treat us like slaves, they treat their dogs and cats so much better. They lie on us, they steal our money orders, and write false reports against us. They lie on us, they assault and murder us with the help and assistance of the Federal Bureau of Prisons. They don't want us to help ourselves, they don't want us to leave out alive or without being mentally, spiritually, or physically wounded. Because this is how they have trained each other and how they have been trained. But my fellow prisoners, it is all our own fault. We have the ball, the power in our own hands, but stupidity, racism, hate amongst each other, ignorance and illiteracy, and no unity is our worst enemy. Because we just can't seem to bring ourselves together as one. These Federal prisons have been in existence for over 100 years, yet we as prisoners have never ever brought all ourselves together for a reasonable cause as one, united all over the Federal system as one. My brothers, I am aware of our circumstances, our situations, our environment and sub-human conditions that we endure every single day in these places, this is why I need you to stand with me for change, better and more positive change. My fellow prisoners, time is running out because we simply cannot continue to live as we have been like this for ever. And believe me my brothers, all of you, I know there will be problems. There always is when it's for change, nothing worth sacrificing for ever comes easy and so it will be with this non-violent togetherness. But my brothers, we must stand up for change we must try to help ourselves, we must save ourselves with ourselves and by ourselves as one for change in the drug laws, parole, reasonable good time, better education, better medical care, better treatment, and other things. But I need you all to stand with me, because we all know it's the only way for change. It's the only way things will ever change in this system, and that is only if we all stand together in unity as one for the cause. We must stop this madness of what is happening to us, or many of us will die in here and never be free. My brothers, please will you stand with me and I mean to the very end!!

CHAPTER TWELVE

THE WORLD I LIVE IN - FOUR

Hurt, pained, wounded, and semi unaware of the world from which I came, I entered into another world, a Federal one, unbeknownst of what to expect or what I might find, not knowing that it would be a world and sub-culture that I would not only never forget, but probably cease to exist in, if I never free myself from it. Realizing that only I myself could "Free Me" from the hurt, pain, and wounds that I have inflicted upon myself and by myself, and that no one is to blame for anything that transpired with me, but me and therefore, only I could help me from me. So I went on a journey to capture me from me, to bring me back to me, so that I could one day free me from the other me, and allow the public and the American people to see and witness that even the guy that was once so many things, could one day rehabilitate himself into one thing, a positive and constructive human being. So while incarcerated, not only do I study law, but I read a great deal, and keep my body physically in shape. I pray a lot, and I take college courses and have degrees and diplomas from colleges and institutions. I stay positive and constructive no matter what the situation and circumstances. Because I know from the very staff that a triple high security Federal lock-down penitentiary like Marion, and ADX Florence, Colorado, was awaiting any negativity from my actions. And because I knew this and saw it before its existence, I never wanted it to be because it would completely keep me forever isolated. So I chose another path along my journey and directed my energies in another direction. That journey took me to where I am so grateful to be at this moment, which is on a positive path, strictly to "FREEDOM"! I don't see nothing else, but that. Never will I ever see anything but that until I achieve and accomplish it or die trying. I live in a world trapped in many semi-subcultures of other prisoners, many of them, themselves lost in a maze, difficult to comprehend, and afraid to stand firm and strong for themselves because they are hopeless, and powerless, by fear and manipulation from other prisoners and the administration. Hindering each other from and for better, positive and constructive opportunities, because they (prisoners) won't stand as one together, not even for the sole genocide of each other. Yet wanting the American public upon their release to think that they tough guys, straight gangsters and serious thugs. But what the public does not know is that they are faking, at least 99% of them. That one percent that are not faking, is as high as I can get based on my observations and my 23 years of experience in these prisons. I live in a world where life means relatively very little among those that live with me. Every day I wake up, I must be prepared for physical battle, stabbings, and murder is usually on the menu along with a knife fight for dessert in these places. Sounds funny doesn't it? But I mean every word of what I'm saying. I only live here because I have to! Because I must in order to hopefully one day see "FREEDOM" in a free world. Rather than through looking up at the sky, or on t.v. or through a prison fence, or by talking about it on the telephone or in a movie. I live in this world because it's the only one at this moment and for the last 23 years that will allow me to exist. I've been in it so long, that I can no longer seem to feel the pain, and hurt, that I use to in the very beginning of the bit. I no longer seem to be semi-unaware of anything now. Because through my 23 years of experience, semi-unawareness will get me hurt or murdered. So I've learned to be very aware. Sounds crazy doesn't it? But that's because prison is a crazy place for most of us, including myself. I see, talk, and walk with the mentally ill in these places all the time. They even have some that don't think they are mentally ill, such as myself. Realizing that something has to be wrong with me after surviving in these places all this time I've been incarcerated leads me to believe that I need some kind of psychiatric assistance I would think.

I live in a world that every day I wake up in this place, some days I say to myself, damn!!!! I can't keep living like this. Like what? Like with all the madness around me, all the time. But, I'm here by choice, I could have made better and more constructive choices. I live in a world where 95% of the prisoners don't even go to the law library to at least try to see if they have a legal issue that might just free them. I live in a world where prisoners are so distrustful of each other, so paranoid of one another that they'll "usually believe anything the correctional officers tell them and the prison administration" before they believe each other. But that's because they don't believe in each other and dislike and distrust each other. Yet we have to live together every single day. I live in a world where everything I do is scrutinized by prison officials and, if they disagree with anything about what I'm saying or doing, they lock me down for as long as they want even if it means violating their own rules and regulations. I live in this world because I refuse to commit suicide and or to force another inmate to murder or kill me. I live in this world because I'm always believing that I'll leave it through the law library rather than by old age or some medical condition that usually goes astray because the treatment is so poor. My prison comrades won't stand with me for better medical conditions, yet they see what it is and refuse to request better medical assistance, but will go right in the prison units and watch t.v. all day. I live in a world where as As-Sadiq, my good friend from New Jersey, always reminds me that a favor will sometimes kill you faster than a bullet, where in prison they take your kindness for weakness, where you better not try to be yourself and where minding "your own business" or being to yourself will cause negativity against you.

I live in a world where my follow prisoners will team up and group up for a baseball game, or a basketball game, or to watch a soccer game, but won't gang up or stand together for parole, reasonable good time, or for a better education. I live in a world where the most famous gangsters and criminals sometimes can't live here for some personal reason or another and/or because this is not the life they can exist in but for so long, and end up dead or committing suicide.

I live in a world with doctors, lawyers, judges, and even Congressmen who see that they, like any other American citizen, is not above the Law, but just like myself, under the Laws, Statutes, and Constitution of the United States. I live here and I know exactly what I'm saying and there is absolutely no doubt about anything I've said. I live in a world where even on sunny days the sun says, "I'm not shining in that place today." There is just too much death, murder, assault, negativity, and dislike with the people among each other that live in that place, so I'll shine somewhere else for a while and leave those prisoners in darkness, because it seems as though they don't want sunshine or light.   They like instead living in the dark without any sun, because every time I shine my light on them they refuse it as if they don't want the knowledge, the respect, the encouragement, or any positivity for a better future- at least while incarcerated.

I live in a world where all my fellow prisoners do is complain, but do nothing to improve themselves and always wanting something for nothing. Always stealing and taking from each other. Yet still complaining about any and everything. I live here, and I'll always live here forever, if I do not win my case in Court. So I stay focused on any and everything I can when it's in reference to my case in that law library. Because one day I want to walk free out of here, and not with a cane in my hand from old age, not looking old, not seriously mentally ill, but in good shape mentally, physically and spiritually. That is why I do what I do in order to stay the way I am and I'm always trying to improve and do better for and by myself the best I can.

I live in a world where my fellow prisoners use any and every excuse they can, not to improve themselves, not to stand up for themselves, and will say anything to each other that sounds good in order not to defend themselves for a better tomorrow. Yet, they are so foolish to think that the Federal Bureau of Prisons don't already know that my fellow prisoners are afraid to stand for anything positive, and constructive and meaningful, and that's why the Bureau of Prisons do what they do to us prisoners. Because first we are prisoners, second, we mean exactly nothing to society, because to society we are civilly dead, and third, if we don't stand for something, then why should there be any change in this wretched and terribly broken Federal system filled with helpless prisoners that don't themselves believe in change or can't imagine changing themselves. And so refuse to change even if it means for parole, better medical conditions, better educational programs, better communications within the system, better living conditions, and better togetherness with each other (prisoners).

This is the world I live in, this is the world from which I cannot escape unless legally released through the U.S. Courts in America by fundamental errors, which I am constantly seeking and searching for in my case through the Courts. I live here and hopefully it won't be forever. At least I don't plan on it being forever! But, if and/ or until then, I live here in one of America's worst Federal prison systems ever. Here is where I now presently remain until I am "FREE", or I die in that law library trying to be "FREE". , nothing else matters! FREEDOM! FREEDOM! and FREEDOM!!

CHAPTER THIRTEEN

THE WORLD I LIVE IN – FIVE

I try not to think of the coldness and menacing glares I sometimes get from other racist prisoners from whom I am forced to live with every single day. I can't challenge nor attack everyone that does it or looks at me that way. Because then I'll have to explain to my home boys why I was forced to slaughter some of them in which I really never want to, unnecessarily. Because some of my home boys will say has Sly Green gone crazy or something <u>over</u> stares! There is very little sympathy, kindness, and compassion in these prisons for each other, as we continue disrespecting each other. The officers and the administration continue on treating us as inferior human beings because that is so much how we portray ourselves to and among each other. Many of my fellow prison brothers are blind, self-destructive and you simply just cannot reach them, because they are just too racist and too self-destructive with rage too ignorant, uneducated, and stagnated in the past, and can't see the future. All they have on their minds is committing more crimes, rather than trying to improve themselves for a better and more positive future in the event they are released back into society.

I live in this world every day, all day. In my world I am forced to hide my rage that at times threatens to come through my feelings for which are my real feelings that will expose me, but I know that I simply cannot expose myself, because it would be havoc in this place if I ever did. I just have to live with what I see and experience all the time. For many reasons I keep saying to myself, I'm not about to be a statistic in these place.

I'm not getting murdered or hurt in these places and I'm walking out of here in good health without a worry in the world. So whatever I see in these places, and whatever I experience in these places, if it's not about being FREE, then I'm just passing by (family). I'm not about to allow any one nor myself to get myself more time than I already have, unless it's extremely necessary. And if that should ever be, rest assured (family) I am ready for the task, and or the challenge. And I'm standing to the very end.

I live in a world, where some prisoners will never see the light of day ever again. Where life is life, murder is murder, and the assault rate is extremely high. I live in a world where if you get caught faking, you'll end up dead, or hurt, or someone's girl. I live in a world where even though I myself am highly respected, that it only takes one serious mistake, and I'll cease to exist just like any other of my fellow prisoners. I live in a world where police officers, and law enforcement cannot expose who they are, because it would create a blood bath with his own life at stake. They are simply not welcome in these places from which I am in. I live in a world where U.S. Attorneys, and Judges, and these types of people period are totally afraid to say who they are and is in constant fear of you not knowing who they are, because they know these guys in here will slaughter them immediately. I live here, and I know that what I'm saying is not only true, but a fact.

I live in a world where my fellow prisoners don't care anything about the police, the Judges, nor the U.S. Attorney's office, but I also live in a world where a lot of my fellow prisoners have cooperated with them and ratted and snitched and informed on their co-defendants or on others, and if found out about they will suffer the same fate as a Judge, a cop or U.S. Attorney.   I live in this world and I'm living in it right now and I know this world, because I had to know it and learn it in order for myself to survive it. I live in a world where humiliation is written in the script. Where misbehavior reports are 99% of the time fabricated against a prisoner in order to keep him confined in the (BOX) Special Housing Unit for a longer period of time than he should be.

I live in a world where segregation and racism are disgusting and accepted. Where there is so much wrong, injustice, pain, and sorrow that no one cares, nor dare speak out because of the consequences they face from others in this world that they too live in with me. I live here and I know. I live in a world where Martin and Malcolm and George Jackson, would never have approved of my fellow prisoners' conduct and their refusal to stand up non-violently for changes in a very horrific Federal prison system, that so sincerely needs change but do not have the right prisoners to change the slave mentality, barbaric system, that so unfairly punishes its prisoners who do not demand even the slightest bit of change for a more positive and better future.

I live in a world, cluttered with lames and chumps, and straight cowards. Where they kill each other, where they stab each other, where all they do is discuss each other's private and personal hearsay business. Where they are totally afraid of positive change, where they refuse to look at life in a more constructive and positive light. Where they totally just don't care about anything with the exception of a football, a deck of cards, a chess board, Dominos, t.v. and sports all day. I live in a world with a bunch of damn illiterate fools, that love nothing more than to hate each other, and will tell you, they don't want to struggle for change, they don't want to sacrifice for change, they don't want to lock down, and never come out until things change for the better.

I live in a world where my fellow prisoners want everybody else in society to help them, but yet they refuse to help themselves, they refuse to sacrifice themselves for a better future. Because they are self-centered, selfish, egotistical, illiterate and ignorant amongst themselves. I live in a world where my fellow prisoners have already given up on positive and constructive change before they can make it happen. Because they don't believe in themselves. Because all they do is complain and cry, but no action, no progress, no struggle, no defiance, no nothing, but illiteracy, ignorance stupidity, and retardation. They (prisoners) know I know, they know everything I am saying is true. They would rather watch t.v. or remember a rap song, than memorize a math problem to help them acquire their G.E.D. Diploma. They would rather sing all night in their cells then read a history or good educational book.

I live in a world where all my fellow prisoners do is watch everything you do, so they can have something negative to say about you if you make even the slightest mistake. I live in a world where if you are too intelligent, other prisoners hate you and despise you because of your positivity and sincerity in being real. I live in a world where jealousy is every day, where it gets some prisoners stabbed and murdered, checked into the special housing unit (Hole). All because of jealousy amongst each other and that's usually for little or nothing. I live here and if you should ever do any of the things that I was accused of doing at trial and get a conviction and sentenced to a Federal prison, you too will live with me, and see and learn and comprehend the same things that I have stated in this book. In this world from which I am confined for the duration of my natural life, live prisoners from all over the world with different attitudes and personalities and criminal behaviors that you can see comprehend, and read only if you are here. I live here with them and their psychology, and their way of life is that of which is in a world from which I myself have been exposed to the last 24 years of my own life. I said that to say, that hardly anything surprises me now. But there will always be a time here and there where something will happen that does surprise me. It's just like that in these places. I know because I live here. But I keep trying to leave by way of the law library. Because it's a terrible place to live and my access is not one that I like passing out to the outside world.

And those of you who need this book, know that everything I say in it is the truth and nothing but pure truth. So before you commit any crimes think about what I go through every single day in these places. I live in a world of constant negativity, destruction, self-incrimination, jealousy, stealing from each other, killing each other, stabbing and murdering each other, beating and assaulting each other. Constant brutality physically from each other and the administration. Ignorance, stupidity retardation. Remember, now, I live here, but if you listen to me, understand the book for what it is, you'll never have to live here with me, because you'll have lived here in your imagination and comprehended what it is to live in a prison by what I'm saying to you right now.

CHAPTER FOURTEEN

THE WORLD I LIVE IN - SIX

The world I live in has a lot of wisdom within it. Some prisoners spend a lot of time trying to figure out what this prison wisdom is. So that they can survive by it to FREEDOM, and be able to live through their prison experiences by knowing what it is. Because those that don't know what it is and don't master it encounter problems, difficulties, trials and tribulations such as unnecessary fights, about what this prisoner said to that prisoner, one prisoner disagreeing with the other prisoner and a fight erupts, murder, or assault is usually the physical result over a simple argument. The prison wisdom would be never to argue with another inmate because this is usually the resolution. If the average inmate had to think from his cell to the mess hall he would never make it because all we do is argue with each other, and hardly ever think of the consequences behind those fights, over a simple argument. The world I live in says never ask a prisoner for his last, and never accept it if he tries to give his last to you. Because prison wisdom says that is all he has, so don't accept his last. Regardless – whether he insists you accept it or not.

Never leave another prisoner with a misunderstanding, unless it's finalized before walking away, because in these prisons that usually leads to something physical.

When you are working on a guy's case, never argue with him about his case, and/ or what he researched in the case especially when you did the research and he researched nothing at all.

Never tell a prisoner I can win this case. Just say

you have this percentage or that percentage of winning this case from what I researched on it.

Never let a prisoner push you into finalizing and/or doing a case, because you will make mistakes.

Never do a case for a prisoner that all he does is complain to you about everything. Because he'll do the same thing with you about his case.

Never help nor assist a prisoner with a U.S.S. Guideline Section 5K1.1, 18 U.S.C. Section 3553(e) or Criminal Procedure Rule 35(b), or any prisoner that you think or feel that way about from reading his paper work. Because prison wisdom states, 99% of the time you will get yourself seriously hurt, checked into the special housing unit, or possibly murdered. Prisoners will hate and despise you for the rest of your sentence for helping a guy with that type of classification.

Never fear another prisoner and if you do, you better not let him observe that you fear him. Because 99% of the time he's going to use that fear to his advantage against you.

Never show weakness, or be too polite, or too kind or too courteous because prison wisdom states that 99% of the prisoners that exhibit that type of respect to other prisoners always have problems from those prisoners that think they are stronger and more physical, not realizing that you are just being yourself and how you were taught. But in prison it's a totally different life style.

Never speak out of turn to another inmate, because he takes it as a sign of disrespect to his manhood.

Never talk too loud to another inmate, he takes it as a sign of disrespect or that you might think he is weak.

Never back down from a fight from another

inmate, lose or win, because if you do, he might take your manhood from you the first chance he gets or take everything you have physically.

Never stare another prisoner in his eyes, unnecessarily, because it usually leads to physical problems.

Never be yourself unless you can represent being yourself. Otherwise, be very serious, very real, very prepared to be very physical at all times, because being yourself and minding your own business, and being by yourself is usually a problem in prison because you are not living in a normal environment with normal people. Criminals. Therefore, you play by the criminal elements, and criminal rules of wisdom. It's the only way to survive in these places.

Never ever turn your back on your home boys when they are battling physically against another state, or group. Always fight to the death with them. Prison wisdom says from my experience of seeing it, that if you don't, they'll find you after it is all over, and probably murder you, rather than just assault you.

Never complain about doing time in the special housing unit. Your fellow prisoners will call you weak, and sometimes tell you, you might tell something on someone because you can't even do your own SHU time.

Never lie to another prisoner about his case. Always be very honest and truthful.

Never get too close to any prisoners while serving time. Because they will exploit your friendship. Not all of them, but 90% of them will, usually when you get into an argument with them.

Everything you ever told or said to them usually will come out at some time or another.

Never tell another prisoner about your very personal problems, 90% of them can't hold water.

Never be too generous to another prisoner, 90% of them take it as a false sign of weakness.

Never get too close to any prison staff just to be close to them, because you are going right to the SHU, checked in by other prisoners. Because the other prisoners will look at that as you being a rat or snitch or informer.

Never get caught lying to other prisoners because then you'll never be believed nor trusted by any of them.

Never think you are better than the next prisoner in anything. Just be a prisoner and you'll encounter less problems then you would ever expect to.

Never disrespect another prisoner about anything at all intentionally, nor deliberately because it could cost you your life for frontin.

Never be unsanitary in prison, always keep your hygiene up, and your cell neat. Because other prisoners will despise your uncleanliness and unhealthy hygiene as being unsanitary.

Never allow nor let any prisoners take advantage of you or use you because they will never stop. They will take it as a sign of weakness and use you to death.

Never ever be prejudiced toward another prisoner. Regardless of his ideology, just make him respect you. Because at the end of the day that's all that matters, is "RESPECT".

Never speak out of turn when communicating with another prisoner. Always be very respectful, but gangster at the same time in your character, always standing strong and firm to the very end in whatever you say or have to say. In other words, never ever back down on anything you say, mean what you say when you say it in these places. Or you will be characterized as a joker or wankster. And if you make a mistake in saying something, say it's a mistake and be very honest about making that mistake in what you said. Be clear (Family) or you will lose your character, your respect, and gangster with other prisoners.

Always stay gentlemen gangster (strong and firm) in everything you do in these places or other prisoners will take it as a sign of weakness, and you will be tested until you fall victim, or until you decide to stand up if you make it to standing up after you've shown that sign of weakness.

Remember, Rome was not built in one day with one brick. So always take your time in your thinking so that acting on impulse don't get you forever in these places along with the ones who already have forever. Because they definitely want your company. And they stay doing something stupid, illogical, and yes! definitely unnecessary.

Everything comes in time, but if you are looking for death, in these places that I live in, it will surely come to you, if that's what you're looking for, without a doubt, without question it will hurry right to you. My philosophy tells me so, and it does not fail me at all.

I'm trapped in a world from which I cannot mentally evade. I came into it through only faults of my own from which the law library is my only way out. Now that I am here, I cannot willingly leave when I am ready, unless the courts unlock the door through a special and precious legal key, which I must present in a winning legal brief before them. It is truly my only way out of here for which I strive for every single day that I have been here. And I refuse to give up. I can't, I never will, I can never give up the fight to win my FREEDOM, because the life I presently live in now is one that I never ever want to experience again. And so I keep trying for the FREE world, a world of love, passion, beauty, and everything that I love and will never ever again take for granted.

CHAPTER FIFTEEN

FLASH BACK - ONE

As I was thinking I flashed back to when I first came into a Youth Detention Center on East Ferry Street in the City of New York. I was 14 years old. I was a juvenile charged for a robbery murder offense along with four other guys. I honestly did not understand the seriousness of what I had engaged myself into, because murder was involved. The public was very upset about that case, and I was too young to comprehend their anger over such a very serious mistake I and the four others had made. I pled out, because my Mother forced me to, but I didn't rat, nor snitch on the others. I took it all, but there was another guy on the case about my age and he told all he could about everything he knew. I kept the "G.Code" close to my heart and took my 18 months as juvenile along with not saying a word about anyone else. I flashed again, to when I was sixteen, and I caught a bank robbery and a red barn armed robbery. I went to trial and they blasted me with 7-21 years in a State of New York prison. Still not comprehending the seriousness of nothing I was doing. My oldest brother (Ice burg) was a local legend in the hood, and kept me and my four brothers safe from harms way. He and a guy by the name of J.D. Ubanks were considered to be very serious guys from the hood and I had nothing to worry about no matter what I did, or at least it appeared that way and to me it was.

I flashed again, to the state prisons I had been in on that 7-21 year New York State beef. I reminisced about Ivan Johnson from Harlem, to Chilie and Julius, Butchie Adams, Levey, Shakim, Born Allah, and I thought as I wondered how they were during. I flashed again and again deep into the past about everything that had ever happened to me. I wondered and wondered, will I ever make it out a Freeman this very last time. Do they have me? Yes! They had closed the door completely on me and my future both in the state and in the FEDS. I flashed on my two sons and daughter, and I wondered about them and probably what they were thinking how I had no choice in the matter and had to proceed to two trials. Because I was pressed by the Federal and State Authorities. I wasn't a Cop-out type of guy. I always believed in standing to the very end, no matter what the circumstances or situation was. It's how my brother had taught us never to tell nothing on anyone, stand up, but don't be no fool either, but stand up first until you read the play. That's what I always do, I always stand to the end, if I read the play as a stand up situation.

I flashed again to my Mother, and to my aunt's and family members and said to myself – this time, they might not be there when or if I ever win these cases. I flashed to the days when I was taken down, on the Federal joint and how serious the take down was. A military helicopter came for me this time, and very heavy security. Extremely heavy too. I knew I was not coming out of this one at all when I saw the security. That alone would crush me while on trial. I flashed again and I thought about the Russells and how very good they had been to me, how as even a young nine year old kid, they had always done anything and everything to help me. I felt disappointed in myself at that moment of the flash. I kept right on flashing and flashing until I came back into reality. I thought to myself for a while, how my Mother had passed, my aunts my uncles, my sister, my friends, and I said to myself – damn, if I do ever get myself released, Nach, Capone, Big Blue, DAve Dog, Dee-Dee, Keppie, Cyrus Double "C", Luca, and all of them will probably be gone. I leaned back on my bed with my feet touching the floor, with a gray sweat suit on, my hair cut short, looking to the ceiling and I said to myself – I ain't getting weak, I ain't complaining about nothing, I'm staying in shape physically and in the law library every single day, until I either get released or die trying. I got up off the bed, and I pulled out Chicago Reds Response from the Court and I went right to work on that case, diligently.

CHAPTER SIXTEEN

FLASH BACK - TWO

When you are incarcerated, these people that control the prison's Administration, Federal Bureau of Prisons, in Central Office. They have the exclusive right to murder you, kill you, destroy you, assault you, mentally and physically and a lot of times we do it to ourselves, spiritually, physically, and mentally, so the prisoner's do it for them 99% of the time, but complain when the Federal Bureau of Prisons does it to us legally. You see, we never stand as one in unity for anything and when we do, it breaks down too fast to call it unity. The officers and the Administration are trained professionals to hate you. You are a criminal, not fit for human society. You are an outcast, a disrespect to the American public. You are a liar, a murder, a killer, a con man, robber. You killed one of their relatives, or you assaulted someone they know. Don't trust you under any circumstances at all. Use you for all the information you can get from a prisoner, so they (Administration) will know what's going on in the prison. You are nothing but a criminal. We (the Administration) can do anything we want to a prisoner, "anything" and get away with it 99% of the time, and cover it up. But, remember, it's not them, it's us, because we are our own worst enemy, and we have no unity, no love and respect for each other. As a whole, we lack that togetherness, to stand as one. We hate and disrespect each other because we are from different races, different parts of the world, different parts of the country, different cities, different hoods, different gangs, or because one prisoner has more power and influence in the prison than the other one does, we are completely separated with absolutely no togetherness. Yet, if we stand together for just one year, we would be able to justify our togetherness forever within these American prisons.

I need you to know that we may have been tough guys on the streets, but once you come to prison you have to reprove yourself, reinvent yourself all over again. No matter who you were on the streets, you have to follow the rules of the prison code in these prisons. The prisoners don't care who you were, what you were about. This is a totally different world from the outside world. You are nothing, no gangster, no stand up guy, no tough guy, no nothing until you prove what you are. You can claim to be have been anybody you want, but you have to prove your toughness, your gangsterism, in these prisons I've been to. And if you don't they (prisoners), take total advantage of you completely. I mean it, when I say only the strong survive in these places. The weak get trampled over terribly without sympathy or pity. So if you ever come to one or these places, stand up by any means necessary, win or lose, just stand up. No matter what the situation or circumstances might be. And they will (prisoners) respect you, and give you your props. Only the strong really survive in these places. You meet prisoners here that you would or could never met anywhere else, but in here. They are from all over the world, and I mean that literally.

They say prisons are universities because you learn things in these places that you would never or could never learn or any place else. Now if they are talking about killing, murdering, con games, stick up games, professional burglaries, professional thieves, pimps, doctors, lawyers, a judge here and there, Congressmen here and there, then the answer is YES!!

They say prisons are the school of hard knocks, now if you are talking about fighting, gangsterism, tough guys, learning how to fight, and learning how to be aggressive in all these ways by learning the scenarios of these things and putting them into practice, then I'll say YES! These prisons are prisons of hard knocks.

They say you learn things in prison that you would or could never learn any place else. YES! You'll see that that is true, just by reading this book.

No matter how nice and respectful you are in these prisons no matter that you are minding your own business. Those are the guys that seem to have the most problems. The guys minding their own business, the gentleman polite guy. Because other prisoners look at that as a sign of weakness, cowardness, chumps or lames, or he's nothing. You have to have toughness and viciousness, and gangsterism behind that politeness, and gentleman respect because if you don't you'll end up as prey in these prisons.

CHAPTER SEVENTEEN

FLASH BACK -THREE

I flashed back to the times and days when I couldn't even see the sun shining, the rain falling, not even the clouds. I had been kept locked down everywhere I traveled 23-7, when the FEDS took me down. I was escorted with 8-9 officers and always some brass in a white shirt were with them, calling the shots. I had to go to recreation by myself, on a visit by myself, eat by myself, everything by myself, hidden away by the FEDS in one of their FED holding spots, constantly being transported from one spot to another. When I was sentenced, I was sentenced to one of the worst United States Penitentiaries in the United States. I thought of all the different races and different classes of people I kept seeing once I got into the Bureau of Prisons. How they eat their meals in the mess hall and to how they reacted to each other. It was truly the United Nations in the Federal system, these guys were from all over the world. Once in the mess halls of Leavenworth, Lewisburg, Colorado, Atlanta, and those other prisons I traveled to, I saw things in the mess hall through my observations, that I would never ever forget. I saw how the gangs mingled with each other. I saw how they didn't mingle at times and why and when they did again and why some would never mingle again. I saw how the Wardens, Lt's, and Captains controlled these Federal prisons differently than how the State did in theirs. I also saw how very intelligent the FEDS were too. How they keep control of their prisons. You need to know that there is absolutely nothing dumb or slow or stupid about the FEDS or State Authorities running these prison systems. They know exactly what they are doing and how to do it. The prisoners are the ones that are slow, stupid, and ignorant. Because they are always getting caught at almost everything they do in these prisons. They are always catching more charges, always getting locked in their cells for constant disciplinary problems with each other. Always doing something negative against each other, and then telling the very authorities that they say are hillbillies, and tobacco chewing officers. Those hillbillies and tobacco chewing officers seem to always get their man. They seem to always have so-called seasoned prisoners ratting and telling on each other and doing whatever against each other. They seem to know everything about the prisoners and how to run this system, yet we keep calling them stupid, and dummys, and all those other names, and they keep going right to training, learning this and that, and that and this about you, physically and if necessary murder you and get away with it simply because they are Federal Employees. And yet you (prisoners) constantly talk about them being slow. But did you know they know more about you than you can ever imagine. Did you know they look at all the high profile pictures coming to work every day, all day, did you know they study you, they memorize who you are, they have a profile book, and a high profile book, and that they have to read about a prisoner at least once every 30 days? Did you know they were trained to not believe anything you say, don't trust nothing you tell them, stay three feet away from you at a distance. They write secret memos on you, and if you are a threat to the ordinarily running of the prison to get rid of you or lock you down. There is a lot more, they learn your slang words so they'll know exactly what you are communicating and saying to each other. Yet we as prisoners call these very officers dumb, now that you know that little bit of information who's the dumb one now, who's looking dumb now, us or them! These prison officials have been controlling these prisons for over 100 years and we as inmates have the audacity to say that they are dumb, and don't know what they are doing. It's us as prisoners who don't know what we are doing or how to do it, and we refuse to self check our own, especially when we know they are doing something totally stupid and against our own principles. We as prisoners won't even step to the other prisoner and say Yo! Don't do that, or Yo! My man! That's out of character pal! We are not living like that. 99% of the time all we do is self destruct. I Flashed and Flashed about these things in my mind, and I wondered to myself many times over, what is wrong with these guys (prisoners), don't they see the light, can't they see, and for the ones that can, why are they not saying anything or educating each other as to what is going these prisons. I Flashed to the medical department in the prisons and how inmates are always dying because they never got to the outside hospital on time. How 99% of the officers don't care if you die or not. Because they have been trained to look at you for what they have classified us as, a prisoner, just like a slave, and we don't say or do nothing, we don't even complain unless it's secretly to each other. I Flashed, and I Flashed deep into the prisoner's psyche of how we think, and how a lot of us are afraid to think because we feel it might get us locked down, when it's better to be locked down for better education, better medical, good time, parole, better treatment, than to be locked down all the time for hurting, and killing, and disrespecting each other. I Flashed again, and again, and then I looked up in my bed as I was laying back resting, and I said to myself somebody got to tell this story, so why not me, because I've got nothing to lose by telling the truth. What I'm saying ain't nothing but pure, uncut, raw truth. I'm giving it to you as I Flash and Flash deep into the minds of prisoners like myself and those of others, and how the system is run and controlled. I'd rather stand for something than nothing at all. Then I turned over on my side fell to sleep, hoping as I do sometimes, that this was all just a dream.

CHAPTER EIGHTEEN

FLASH BACK - FOUR

I was walking the yard with my good friend As-Sadiq, and as we were walking, we both flashed back into Attica, New York, and how dangerous and serious the joint was. We spoke about Jose Harris, a New York State prison legend, and how he came in when he was only 17 or 19, years of age, to Com-Stock, New York. And to all of the State High Security joints. Jose Harris, Damanon Shakim Allah, Born Allah, Tom Cross, As-Sadiq, K.O. Smithie, Ivan Johnson, Butchie Adams, Iceburg, Big Booker, Koti, Herman Bell, Jaleal, Anthony Bottom. Those were the names we talked about and reminisced about. As-Sadiq seemed to know them all. I had only had the pleasure of meeting a few of them. But I really liked, appreciated, and respected them all, concerning what I had heard about them. But Jose Harris was always said to be the most dangerous of them all. Born Allah, the most intelligent of them all, and Herman Bell, the most political of them all. Myself and As-Sadiq wondered about how they might be doing as we talked, we hoped that they would one day be released, and hoped that they stay focused on their cases, but a few of them had either made parole or been released through the courts like Born Allah, Ivan Johnson, Big Booker, from Rochcester, New York, and Butchie Adams. I was glad to hear that as I continued on reminiscing with As-Sadiq about those New York State prisons. Then he stopped and said that that Jomo, another legendary figure, had passed away before he had left the New York State system. Jomo, too was a very popular legendary figured to be reckoned with. I asked As-Sadiq, about Big Amar from Brooklyn,

New York, about A-Zar, from the Bronx, about J.J. and Dwight Battles, from Buffalo, New York, and he said they were all doing well, the last time he had seen them. I asked him, were they working on their cases, and he said some were and some were into other things. We flashed on and on, and reminisced deep into the prisons in the state of New York and then he said, you know, Jones passed away in his sleep, and I said, Ya! Shabazz (Bostic) told me that when I was at USP Atlanta. As-Sadiq said, Yea! Man! He died in his sleep and I flashed back into my inner thoughts about some things that had transpired with myself and Jones, and a few of his soldiers, and I said to myself, Dam! Jones is gone! I thought again to myself, about him and when I went to church the next day, I said a prayer for him dead or alive, it made no difference now anymore, because now he was gone forever. Whatever was on my mind could never be and would never be. I thought again for a few moments, as I was walking with As-Sadiq, and he looked at me, and he said Sly Green, from all of what I've heard about you, my friend, you look good, I was thinking, you might be crazy by now, insane, off the chain, out of it completely Sly Green. He smiled and shook my hand and hugged me, while tears came down my eyes like a river. I said Thank You Sadiq. You are the only one in all the 21 years I've been incarcerated that's ever said anything like that to me. Sadiq, you are the only one that feels my pain. I looked at him as in my eyes were running a river of tears and I said, I love you pal! Thank you so much for your sincere kindness and the respect that you have for me. I walked away wiping the tears from my face. From that day on, As-Sadiq became like a brother I had never had in my life. I flashed back to Double "C", Dave Dog, Luca, my own brothers, to Big R., Keylow,

Chancey, Big Blue, Denita, Maryland to Lori, and Tookie, and then I said to myself, he reminds me of them all. Then I suddenly thought of my sister Tracy and I said he's loyal to the death, like her, and when the ten minute move was called, I went to my unit, and I laid down and I took an unusual long rest, never ever forgetting what my good friend As-Sadiq had said to me. Because he brought me back, he gave me more strength, and endurance and peace of mind. He told me in so many words, that Sly Green, you can make it out of here, you are strong, I see it in you. From that day on we have been the very best of friends, loyal to each other to the death. , I do not mind saying I love As-Sadiq to death as well.

CHAPTER NINETEEN

FLASH BACK - FIVE

As I continue to win these cases, with the gift that God has given me. I often Flash Back into the life I was born in, which was a constant struggle of uncertainty, based on the environment I came up in and the imagines of those I saw constantly around me. I molded myself into them, not knowing at such a very young age, what I was doing would someday lead me into State and Federal penitentiaries for the rest of my natural life. Yet, I have no complaints because I could have stopped at any time and went on and became a lawyer, but the street environment had already poisoned me severely, especially based on what I was seeing in those streets at such a very young age. I just couldn't pull myself away from the streets. I loved them, nothing else in the world meant so much to me, other than those streets. I can't complain, I can't hold anyone responsible for my own wrong doings. Whatever happened with me, was because of me. Like now, I've transformed myself strictly into doing Law, I love everything about it. It's all I like doing. I can't sit around watching t.v. unless it's about the courts or something to do with something important. I can't waste my time in the prison yard all day, unless, it's about law. I have to go to the law library as much as possible. Because my life so much depends on it.

I look at my fellow prisoners and they sit around watching t.v. with sentences of 10, 20, 30 years, life terms, multi life terms, and all 90% of the 1700 want to do is watch t.v., watch sports, play chess, play cards, and other games and refuse to go to the law library. Honestly, some of them have never been to the law library. They won't even help themselves, they won't even try to research their own cases, or learn how to. The worst thing you can do is try to get some of them to try to help themselves, they will turn on you like a dog, and want to fight you for trying to help them. They simply refuse to do anything at all and they don't want you helping them either. This applies to 90% of them. You'd have to see it for yourself to believe it.

I find myself Flashing Back all the time, about why won't they stand together for change, why won't they stand together for Freedom, for a better environment, for togetherness. Nothing violent, non-violent togetherness. Don't they see that they will never ever be free until they effect change, unless they stand up for change as one. I just don't understand why they (prisoners) don't want to help themselves, to a better future. How is it that they get up every day, never thinking of change, always under pressure, always in fear of each other and the system, always wanting nothing for a better future. Is there something wrong with me, for wanting for my fellow prisoners, what I want for myself? Is there something wrong with me for asking them to please take a look at what is happening to us? How it is going down? How it will always go down if we don't stand up for change. It is unreal how we allow ourselves to be treated in these places. It is unreal how we do what we do every day in these places and do not stand together for a better and more positive future. I'm advocating non-violent togetherness for a better future, under sub-human conditions, in a terrible environment, where it appears that 90% of my fellow prisoners like living in. And will not do anything at all to help themselves to a better future and always appear to have an excuse why they cannot affect a non-violent change in these sub-human environments that we are so constantly subjected to every single day with constant pressure under dire conditions, not fit for human living.

CHAPTER TWENTY

FLASH BACK - SIX

After reading a case, I was sitting on my bed, looking at the ceiling and I Flashed Back into the prison system. I said to myself, we as prisoners, African Americans, Hispanics, Native Americans, and Poor Whites will always suffer in this system and be subjected to the sub-human conditions that we endure and are faced with in these prisons every day, as long as we continue to rat and snitch on each other, oppress each other, disrespect each other, murder, kill, assault, and harm each other, while not looking out for the well being of each other. As a prisoner, and other prisoners we live in a world plagued with disrespect against each other in almost every way that you can possibly think of.

Even me, myself, no matter how many prisoners I free from these prisons, the mass majority of them do not appreciate it, nor do most of them even take it seriously because usually they come right back. They simply do not value their FREEDOM, as some of us have learned to do. It's a bitter pill to swallow, it's amazing how we as prisoners compromise our Freedom and oppress ourselves along the way. It's a shame how we as prisoners live in a prison society within a culture, where the norm is murder or be murdered, stand up or die, you cannot falter or you will definitely pay the price. Brutality and assaulting one another mentally, physically, and even spiritually is the norm in these places. I live in a world within a world that you would never even imagine what's it's like to live in unless you are a prisoner. I live in a world where life is of very little value, where you lose yours for saying the wrong thing to another prisoner, where even looking at another prisoner in the wrong way will get you assaulted or murdered. I live in a world where you die for just touching the t.v., or telephone, or stepping in front on the other prisoner in the mess hall lines. I live in a world where there is very little respect for each other, where racism is at its highest, where if you show one sign of weakness, and it's seen by the wrong prisoner, you pay the price however he deems it appropriate. I live in a world that I've become numb to, a world filled with constant altercations and a routine of difficulties. I live in a world where some prisoners love it here and would rather live here than to be FREE. I live in a world where, failure, and conflicts are always a part of life.

I live in a world where it's extremely dangerous, and yes, difficult to survive, but in order for me to one day be FREE, or die trying, I must myself continue to endure the bumps, the stumbling blocks, and hurdles that get in my way at times or I'll never ever be FREE! So I live the way I do because I must not and cannot give up, no matter what the circumstances, and conditions turn out to be, I must endure, I can never ever raise the flag of surrender. Because I live in a world where I must succeed in winning by FREEDOM, or it will surely gaffle me up completely into death, for that is the only other alternative to which I have in the world from which I presently live in.

CHAPTER TWENTYONE

FLASH BACK - SEVEN

I was standing one early morning in the laundry room looking out the window, the sun was bright, and I knew it was going to be another one of those hot June summer days in Florida. As I was looking at the grass and trees, a distance away, I gazed up in the morning sky and Flashed Back into the past. I thought to myself, for the millionth or more time, how could some of those whom I had taken to be so loyal, as my friends, and even family to me, cross me, lie on me, hate me, despise me, and want nothing more than to see me disappear off the face of the earth forever or never to be seen ever again. As I Flashed deeper into the depth of my thoughts, still gazing at the light blue morning sky, I wondered why did they feel that way about Sly Green. I had been extremely generous and very gentlemen-like to them all that were on the witness stand trying to place me forever in Federal and State prisons for the rest of my natural life and if possible the death penalty too. I thought hard about how powerful the American Government really is. The money they would pay witnesses to say whatever they wanted them to say or rehearsed them into saying. I thought how the Government would buy them a new house, new everything, even a new life if it meant putting Sly Green away for the rest of his life. I thought about Yummy, Santana, Robert Felder, Derrick Leonard, Howard Doran, Judy Spidell, Norman Workman and even James Wright and Steven Brown, whom I had never seen nor ever met in my entire life. I thought deeply too! Why? How could James Wright and Steven Brown fabricate a story against me, just to get their charges dropped?

The Court knew this, the prosecution knew this, but without those two on the state case there would have been no case. So I realized that even lies will go for a conviction. It wasn't a matter of guilt or innocence, it was a matter of whoever told the best lie would win the case or whoever performed the best. Then I Flashed to my Federal case, and I thought about it again and again as I always do, and I thought about why Yummy, and why would you do something against a guy that loved and cared so deeply about her and, why Judy, would you do it period, more so than any of the others. I thought about how Norman took it all as if it was a joke to him because he felt he was safe like Kevin Green, my own cousin whom also had testified against me with half truths and lots of fabrications. Both he and Norman had played the Federal witness program. I thought of Felder, and said to myself, I looked out for you, when you were down and needed favors, and this is what I got in return, a Federal witness against me. I thought of Derrick, and I just didn't see him coming with the cross, but there he was. I said to myself Double "C" would never go out like Derrick and I was right, Double "C" held up to the very end strong and firm all the way with me. I thought of Duran, and Santana, (Nebbitt Lee) and Willie Thomas, (Friutbelt crab), and I said, Damn, I can't believe this. There they were testifying against me for their own benefit, for reasons of their own. I thought about the Racketeering Enterprise charges I was up against, the Super King Pin Act I was up against, the conspiracy I was up against, the Title 21 U.S.C. Section 841(b)(1)(A),(b)(1)(B), Section 843 witness tampering, extortion, kidnapping, organized crime period, murders, assaults, money laundering, phone counts, attempted murders, everything to do with organized crime, they charged me with it, in a 73 count indictment along with 32 others. As I was reminiscing, and thinking deeply I steered into another zone. I wondered, I pondered deep into my psyche, and I came to the conclusion, that not even I, myself, could have made any of them stand up once they saw and seriously realized that the government, and the judge together were in together to bring me down by any means necessary. I realized that once even they knew that I was being transported by military personnel at times and by military helicopter, that I was not coming out of this. They flipped. They turned. They rolled and did what they did because they said to themselves, that Sly Green will never ever walk away from 25-to-life for the State of New York, and 4 life terms, plus 110 for the FEDS, with a total of 5 life terms, plus 135 years for both the state and FEDS. I reminisced deeper and deeper about it, and as I was coming up out of that deep maze in thought, I said to myself, as I usually do when I'm Flashing Back like this, I said damn! I got to win. I got to come out of this madness. I am not staying forever. I've got to win! Family! I've got to! and as I was walking out of laundry room with a semi-distant look on my face, dressed in a pair of white knits, low tops, white socks, a gray shirt, and green Federal khakis, Money Clip, a guy from Tampa, Florida, was walking into the doorway as I was coming out, he looked at me, and said, Yo! Sun! You alright this morning? Suddenly I looked up with my eyes staring into his, and I said, I'm Frosty! Clip! And I kept it moving until I got to my room, I opened the door, sat down on the bed with just myself being alone, and I went back to reminiscing about something else. It's what I do, at times with all the time I was sentenced to, it keeps me thinking, reminiscing, and Flashing Back and forward, and always Zoning from here to there or from there to there. It's something I always seem to find myself doing.

And then I got up, and I went into my legal bag, I pull out the Doctor's case, the one Roy Black had represented on appeal, and won, and then Doc couldn't afford to rehire him again and had gotten convicted, and sentenced to 30 years in Federal prison. I started looking again at Doc's case, because As-Sadiq, the head of our Firm, had assigned me as the point man on the case. I started looking at what I could and or possibly could not do for Doc. In other words, I was back into the real world, and out of the maze, I so often fall into when I'm thinking and reminiscing deep into the past, or far into the future. It keeps me focused and balanced.

CHAPTER TWENTY-TWO

FLASH BACK - EIGHT

Suddenly Doc, decided a few weeks later, that he wanted another prisoner to take his case, but he thanked the Firm for what it had done for him, but that he felt more comfortable with the other jail house pro-se litigant working on his case. We thanked Doc, and informed Doc, that jail house pro-se litigants are like doctors, such as himself. If you don't like one doctor, you can always go to another one. It's your choice Doc, we told him. Doc took what paperwork we had, and went on. I honestly felt somewhat pained while looking at Doc, because he appeared to be suffering from some mental disabilities or depression, suppression and the refusal to accept the fact that he had been given 30 years in a Federal prison. The times I spoke with Doc and walked the yard with Doc he was always saying that the government and the courts had criminalized medicine. I told Doc that he should never had pled guilty to 30 years in a Federal prison at the age of 60 years old, and even though he had pled involuntarily, unintelligently, and unknowingly, that he still had a chance to give his plea back. Because he had involuntarily pled under extreme stress, duress with the threat of the government arresting his entire family, if he did not plead guilty. I had explained to Doc that I and the Firm could win this case for him. But, there were other prisoners in his ear for whatever reasons, and I told Doc, we don't solicit clients Doc, our clients come to us, when and if they choose to do so.

A few days later I saw Doc in passing and I very politely said hello to Doc, and very politely kept it moving. We went on to our next case, while hoping the best for Doc and his future.

The next case, I asked the Firm could I have a leave of absence for two months, so I could personally help and assist my friend Michael Johnson from Chattanooga, Tennessee. He had a gun charge and drug charges. We both did his Title 28 U.S.C. Section 2255 motion/petition/memorandum of law. We put fourteen issues together, and submitted them to the court. We are presently awaiting a response.

The next case was a case for a guy by the name of Jammie Toby, his case was a 2255 motion as well, two issues concerning a major drug conspiracy in West Palm Beach. It was about his being enhanced to career offender status, based on improper State of Florida priors, for career offender status, based on Florida State statute Section 893.13/893.101. I felt that his state predicates were inappropriate for career offender status. Because the Florida State Statute Section 893.13, lacked "mens rea" for the illicit nature of the substance in violation of Descamps v. United States, 133 S.Ct. 2275 (2013); Donawa v. U.S. Attorney General, 735 F.3d 1275 (11th Cir. 2013); and Sarmientos v. U.S. Attorney General, 2014 U.S. App. LEXIS 2650 (CA 5th Cir. 2014). The two state drug priors that I contested in this case were drug priors from 2005/2006/ and were state priors, he was arrested for rather than what he had pled guilty to. I stated that not only were they not eligible for career offender status, but that they also violated Shepard v. United States, 544 U.S. 13, 26 (2000); modified categorical approach/ Taylor v. United States, 495 U.S. 575 (1990). Because they lacked Shepard material such as his state prior transcripts, state prior plea colloquy, and state prior indictments or sentencing transcripts from the state. I also raised an issue about the guy not being able to appeal that he had involuntarily, unintelligently, and unknowingly waived his appeal rights away because counsel told him that he had none based on the fact he had agreed to waive them away. I explained to the court that the guy's 200 month sentence had exceeded a sentence permitted by the U.S.S. Guidelines, and the U.S. Congress, based on his unconstitutional career offender status. The Government has yet to reply.

We go on and on with taking and winning and sometimes we lose one every now and then. But no matter what the situation or circumstances might be, we put our best into our cases. We do this legal work as much as humanly possible. You would have to be insane to sit around in prison all day watching t.v., playing games, or watching sports, and you are serving a 30 year sentence. But a lot of prisoners do just that. They simply won't try to help themselves. They really try to do the 30 years, the 20 years, the 15 years, or the ten years, or five years or life sentence not doing anything at all. You would have to see it for yourself to believe it. There are very few prisoners that go to the law library at one time, about 30 will usually go to the law library at once, since my 23 years of incarceration of 1700 prisoners or even out of the many prisoners. The most I've ever seen at once is about 50, and that's only because a new case or Supreme Court case or new law has surfaced. Even then, you'll see them for a few days, never ever to see them again. When I see things like this, some prisoners will say to me, what do I expect, 86 of the Federal inmates have cooperated with the government or their cases against their co-defendants. That's why a lot of them out of 219,000 do not go to the law library. There is no reason for them to. But they have all other kinds of reasons why they claim they won't go themselves. So at times when I Flash Back into my memory of the past, I often say to myself, that they (prisoners) won't stand up because there are only certain prisons a lot of them can go to. They won't stand up because some correctional officers do and will expose them and their pass. They won't stand up because they feel they can't stand up or they will be found out about when they don't want to risk themselves, nor their lives, and personal security of themselves to others. Because they have heard so much about what happens to those who end up being found out about on their cases. This stops a lot of prisoners from standing together firmly for various important cases. This prevents a lot of unity among prisoners, because they don't trust each other because of these types of situations with their fellow prisoners, especially when they find out about each other. This is what keeps us separated, fighting, and killing and assaulting each other. We live in an imperfect environment and these types of situations with each other prevent us from being as one in unity. Prisoners sometimes lose their lives when they are exposed about what is in their paperwork. When they go to these Federal penitentiaries they have to show their paperwork or stay in the special housing unit where they will be hidden from the prison population, because the other prisoners will not allow them to live among them if they know positively for sure that another prisoner has ratted and or snitched on his case. Prisoners have an unquenchable thirst for violence and revenge for those who are snitches, and for those who are timid and weak. Sometimes other prisoners misread the situation or the other prisoner's personality as being timid and weak. And gets himself murdered, seriously assaulted and yes taken completely off the planet for his own demise.

They (prisoners) go to war in these prisons, they move out in large groups to assault, murder, and kill each other by any means necessary. If you are from where they are from you better be with them because when it's all over with and you were not with them when they needed you most, they are going to do whatever they deem your punishment appropriate to be. In other words, you have got to get down with them unless you have a very good excuse as to why you did not or was not present with your homeboys, or the crew you are with.

CHAPTER TWENTY-THREE

FLASH BACK - NINE

The life I live is of no effort without error and short comings. Therefore, no matter what I do in this system, if left unchecked will continue as it continues to be, which is a system of slaves, degenerates, and fools without a cause, and much worse. I live in a very dangerous society every single day, faced constantly with trials and tribulations, subjected to sub-human conditions. I'm constantly around prisoners that refuse to stand up for themselves under an oppressive and suppressive prison system, that bares us no respect, and treats us like slaves.

I live in a world where my fellow prisoners won't stand up for anything at all, but the prison count and they do that only because they are afraid of being confined to the special housing unit 23-7. I live in a world where my fellow prisoners are afraid to win and succeed because they are so terrified of the system and would rather disrespect each other than to band together as one for a great cause. I live in a world where I don't mind failing for standing up for better conditions, but where my fellow prisoners won't stand with me with strength in numbers. Because the system does not respect us, nor do we try to make them either, because we fear it, we are simply afraid of the repercussions that follow behind for standing together. Some days when I walk into the mess hall, the thought of standing on the table comes to me, to stand before my fellow prisoners and scream as loud as I can at the top of my voice, my brothers, all of you, what is wrong with you, why do you not ask for change, why do you not request for better this and better that, and to be treated as human beings rather than like slaves and animals in chains? My brothers, please! Stop fighting against each other, stop disrespecting each other, stop doing negative things to one another and stand together as one in unity for one cause, for us all as one. And if we fail as one, then we will have failed together and did not stay timid and weak against an unjust, cruel, and dangerous system, that hurts, assaults, and kills us at will and gets away with it 99% of the time. But I can't scream these words out to my fellow prisoners, because they will say I'm crazy and that I've been incarcerated too long, that I've lost it. And pass me off as an emotional disturbed triple O.G. that can no longer function on a normal level. Because I'm tired of seeing all the wrong and terrible things being done to my brothers, all of them. And them doing wrong to themselves for whatever reasons we do to each other.

In this world I live in, you can't dress as you wish, nor say what you want, or think. I live in a place where some people spend the rest of their lives in prison for crimes they have never committed or for a conspiracy charge, they never knew anything about. I live in the greatest country in the world with one of the most dangerous prison systems on earth, a system that murders and kills its own prisoners without just cause. A system that is rotten to its core. A system that will deliberately, intentionally, and wrongly violate your entire family on criminal conspiracy charges, knowing they have absolutely nothing to do with the conspiracy, but only to get your family and or friends to get you isolated for multi years of your life in a Federal prison for anything and or usually for drugs the weight of a nickel, or no more drugs than can fit into a coffee cup.

I live in a country where racism in the criminal justice system is rampant and steadily against people of color, especially against African Americans, even though they are not responsible for not even half of the crimes committed in this country according to the Federal Uniform F.B.I. Crime Statistics on a yearly basis. I live in a country where the criminal justice system is skewed toward the convictions of people of color intentionally and deliberately. Where the Federal Bureau of Prisons Central Office Directors are known for saying don't give em nothing and keep your foot on their necks as long as the prisoners allow it to stay there. I live in a prison system where according to the Bureau Director, if they (prisoners) are not protesting or complaining or afraid to stand up for themselves, then they (prisoners) must be satisfied with how they are living and how we are treating those slaves, animals, and misfits, because that's exactly what they (Federal Authorities) call us to our faces and behind our backs.

I live in a country and prison system, where if my brothers would just be as I call them all, my brothers, and respect each other, as such, then we could have parole, reasonable good-time, better education, better treatment, and better respect for each other. But for many stupid and ignorant reasons my brothers continue day in and day out for the last 23 years, to continue on the useless journey and path that they continue to travel unnecessarily based on stupid and ignorant reasons that defy not only logic, but even basic human principles, that when seen and examined by the outside world, looks exactly like what we are, a bunch of damn fools, murdering, killing, assaulting, and destroying each other.

CHAPTER TWENTY-FOUR

FLASH BACK - TEN

I was sitting in my cell after reading a case on law at about 10:00 in the evening, I Flashed Back into a distant memory of the past thinking deeply of Lori, and how good she was to me for all of those years. I wondered how she was doing? Was she still nursing? Was she still beautiful? Did she age any? Was she still so sweet and dressing so very pretty? I thought about her sons and daughters, how very good that she raised her four kids. How they all turned out so very successful in life. I pondered in my mind, why would anyone not want me to have such a God's gift as Lori in my life forever? And then I came to the conclusion that they too must have seen all the wonderful things in her that I did too, or that they saw some of them and wanted her in their life, or that whoever the guy is, she likes him or because my name is Sly Green, or that she believed everything they said about me but finally they got to my Lori, and convinced her that they knew me and they convinced her, that I was not the one for her. That I was simply all the wrong things for such a very nice person as herself. Or that, I've got extremely too much time and Lori, you will never be able to ever be with him ever again. I wondered even what they may have said at times because I knew in my heart whoever they were, they were out for themselves to get her. To be with her, so it was mandatory to lie, criticize and hate on me. Because they would have to say and do anything to erase me out of her memory. I wondered and I wondered, but I couldn't call because I didn't feel her anymore like I once did deeply. I couldn't look at all the photos of her I had, because I had hidden them away totally out of my existence. All I could do is think here was a lady I loved with all my heart and soul, as I did no other ever in life with the exception of Tookey (Vician Heard), and she flipped right over on me, turned on me, just simply one day crossed me out. I said to myself! Damn! Those lames finally did it, they finally took the one I loved with all the life I had in me. I thought of Tookey and the deep love and respect she had always endured and showed to me, and how I had loved het too. I thought of Yummy, but that wasn't for long, nor Judy either. I Flashed on Lisa, and Flashed right by her in my thoughts in passing. I Flashed on Denita and I said to myself, how could she believe any and everything told to her so easily, without logic or proof, without any substance to the stories. I wondered about Sonya and how I hadn't seen her in so long, and I Flashed until I became exhausted. I got up from the table desk, I was sitting at. I looked directly at the wall in front of me and I said to myself, these are the consequences of being confined in prison. You lose your best friends, your girl friends, those you love, and you wonder and wonder some days until you just don't feel like wondering. I stopped staring at the wall. I got up and sat on my bed, put my ear phones on and went to 90.7 FM NPR radio world news station. I stayed on it for a few hours, and fell asleep wondering what tomorrow might bring me. Because it's all I can hope for, is tomorrow, the next day, always, hoping and searching for another day. Always!

CHAPTER TWENTY-FIVE

SURVIVING

I came into the Federal Joint thinking I might just have to assault, murder, and/or kill someone in order to survive around so many other gangsters, killers, murders, stickup guys, con men, and thieves. You name it, they are here on a high profile level too. Whatever you imagined in the underworld of becoming, they are here. But I went straight to the law library. I went thinking I could help my lawyers help me. But that was not to be. They were not listening to anything I had to say at all. But as time went on, I would learn from the other prisoners that if you wanted out, you had better do the best you can to get yourself out. In other words learn the law yourself and help yourself to help yourself to "FREEDOM". That I did, with the help of so many other Jail house pro-se litigants. I walked a path of law, I went on a journey of law, searching and learning until one day six years later I got it to where I felt I could one day free myself. Ever since I got it at Florence, Colorado, I've never ever stopped trying to free myself. I feel good too, I feel strong and firm. I'm not saddened, I'm not hurting, I'm not upset or angry at anyone. I'm Sly Green to the very end.

I'm just trying to win my FREEDOM like any other rational prisoner should be doing. It hurts me terribly when I'm in the law library 90% of the time with just a very few prisoners in it. Yet many prisoners are serving life terms, 30 years, 20 years, 15 years, and 10 years for drugs only. Especially in the Federal penitentiaries. Racism is rampant in the judicial system and those that it is perpetrated against don't seem to care in the least. They pretend to act as if they have been treated fair. Knowing that the color of their skin got them a longer sentence. Here I was with 5 life terms plus 135 years both state and Federal. I never complained not once, but I've learned what it takes to win and that if I don't win, then I'll never ever be free again. I see some right now and as I work my case, I expect it to get brighter, and if it doesn't, well I'll never know because I'll has deceased trying. You can't give up no matter how much time you have. You have to at least try to win, at least see if you can win, and stay trying, stay seeing or you'll end up dead in these places or with more time or on suicide watch or in a prison mentally ill ward. You have to stay focused on your FREEDOM. Because you never know what might happen for you.

When I file cases in the Courts for other prisoners, I've come to the realization that the northern courts such as the First Circuit, the Second Circuit, the Third Circuit, they are so much more conservative than the Eleventh Circuit, the Ninth, and the Sixth Circuit. The Seventh Circuit is okay, the Eighth is good, the Tenth is good, but the Ninth is by far the best and fairest of them all. The Eleventh is very good and not as racist as the prisoners keep saying it is. It's a very good circuit to me and for my cases. The Fifth Circuit and the Fourth Circuit are terrible and extremely racist. They are the two worst circuits especially the Fourth Circuit. I've tried cases in all of them too. As for the D.C. Circuit, it's fair, it's okay. No one can change my mind because I've just stated exactly how I see them, I've been in all of them, and my name is on cases in every last one of them or it should be by now unless a prisoner tells me not to put my name on the cover of his paperwork, because some of them tell me not to.

I've filed so many cases in the U.S. District Courts, that I know the Judge's names and their background and how they usually decide in the court.

I've read and researched so many District Court cases, that I have a very good estimation of which ones will usually give you justice and which ones will not. I study the Judges in all the courts. I research who they are. For example, Ms Kovakavich, in the Middle District of Florida, Tampa Division is one of the worst Judges I've ever encountered in my filings. That Judge is not only racist, but she hates prisoners period. Anything the government says, she goes with it. She is not a fair Judge at all. The same for U.S. District Court Judge Susan Bucklew, in the U.S. District Court for the Middle District of Florida, Tampa Division. Mr. Hurley, the U.S. District Court Judge in the Southern District of Florida, he's not racist, nor is he not fair, that is why they called him "Hang em High Hurley," a name given to him when he was on "60 Minutes" some years back when he said he would sentence people until he reached one million years in Prison for indicted individuals. He is a good Judge from my filings to him, but others may not see him the same way as I see him. U.S. District Court Judge Michael Moore of the Southern District of Florida, a straight racist and believes everything the government tells him, and is terribly unfair to prisoners and their filings to his Court. Judge Gold Southern District of Florida is very fair and a gentleman, and highly respected by all Federal prisoners and I hope one day that he is nominated to the U.S. Court of Appeals, based on his fairness and impartiality.

The U.S. District Court Judge in the Southern District of New York, Gleesson, is a very fair Judge, and I hope he gets nominated to the U.S. Court of Appeals and then to the Supreme Court one day. U.S. District Court Judge in the Southern District of Florida, Ms. Cook, a very nice and very fair to all people. I honestly hope she gets a nomination to a higher court one day. It's a shame how the Judges know a lot of times, that the government is lying and fabricating a case against you and they agree with them, and blame it on your counsel. And there you are in a Federal prison for the rest of your entire life, on a bogus conviction, that they knew from the very start. It's a shame how afraid we as citizens are of our government. And the fear it put into the American people. You can't help but see it when you are incarcerated. You have prisoners in these Federal prisons serving life terms for drugs the weight of a nickel, and some serving multi-life terms for drugs that cannot fill a small coffee cup. You have people in Federal prisons, a lot of them too, for conspiracy charges that they don't know anything at all about and was not conspiring with anyone, but was just a friend to a person whom the government threatened that if you don't testify against the person being charged, you are going down with him or her. You have people in Federal prisons for made up conspiracies by the government that were never conspiracies at all. The government simply made them up. The government simply created them on their own as they do with 99% of their conspiracy cases. The Judges know this in advance because they help them create them against you. The F.B.I., the D.E.A., the U.S. Attorneys all are altogether against you by any means necessary, whether you are innocent or not, they do not care. When I say they'll take your whole family down on a conspiracy, I mean exactly that. They'll do that knowing that your family members are innocent, but they want to flip them on you and if they don't flip on

144

you, lie on you or say what the government wants them to say, then they'll be in a Federal prison with a trumped up Federal Title 21 U.S.C. Section 846, serving 10, 20, 30, or a life sentence for not testifying against their own family member or against an honest friend. Now, if you don't believe what I'm saying, then just visit these Federal prisons, or check the person's transcripts or investigate what I'm saying and you'll be amazed. When I say there are a lot of Federal prisoners serving 10, 20, 30 years, life and multi-life terms for drugs the weight of a nickel, and not enough to even fit in a coffee cup, I mean it and if you don t believe me, check it out the way I just explained how you can. I know these things personally because I do cases, I read my clients' cases, I study them, I'm a prisoner just like they are, and when I do their cases along with the Firm, I put my heart into it. What I've just said to you, I see it all the time, it's only beginning to slow down a little somewhat because of President Obama and the prejudice and racism he sees in these drug laws. 10. 20, 30 years, and life terms with absolutely no drugs at all. The worst thing though about all of this is a lot of prisoners know these things are true as well. All they do is watch t.v., watch sports, play cards, it's as if they are in a deep sleep, or they just don't care, because I know they see the same things I'm seeing. They have got to, because they are right here with me. That fear thing about being left in the cells and not getting out for months, scares my fellow prisoners to death, they just can't stay in their cells for a good cause to save their own lives from disaster, from ruin. They just don't want to stand up for nothing, and like I said in the other chapters, the only reason they stand up for the count is because they are afraid they will be isolated in the Special Housing Unit for not standing up for the count. Things could have changed for the better, years and years ago, but these prisoners simply refuse to help themselves. And they tell everything on each other and even on a correctional officer for trying to help them. They tell on the very person that tried to help them help themselves. You have got to see this madness and twisted illogical way of prisoner thinking for yourself. And for those of you that happen to read this book, I'm hoping that you won't ever expose yourself nor your friends, nor anyone that you care about to this type of environment, these conditions, this way of life, because you will never be the same again, and nor will they. But it's not impossible on the other hand to change and rehabilitate yourself. Because that is exactly what I had to do after seeing all of this madness. And I feel great about my rehabilitation because it's something I had to do in order to get to where I am now in my life.

CHAPTER TWENTY-SIX

CHANGE IN THE SYSTEM

When I first entered into the Federal system over 20 years ago, prisoners stood up for better conditions, things were so much better. Then approximately 10 years or so later, a different breed of prisoners started coming into the system. They were younger, weaker, and dumber. They had no morals, ethnics, or principals about themselves. They were rats, and snitches, and dirty without any money, and they were broke, and sentenced for petty crimes. They were mostly gang members and they had no self-respect for themselves, nor for others. Most of them were simply petty criminals that the Federal system had never tolerated before. The FEDS became just another state system. The Federal prisoners today simply don't stand up for anything. They don't even control themselves 90% of the time. These prisons are controlled by the correctional officers, and administration. These Federal prisoners don't control anything at all in these prisons and they know it. They are too afraid to stand up, they are weak minded, afraid of the consequences of what follows behind standing up for themselves. They have no unity at all among each other. They hate each other, they despise each other. They steal from each other, they snitch on each other, they kill, murder, and assault each other. They don't trust each other, they are geographical against each other. They rape each other. They don't trust each other. They are racist against each other. They go to court and they testify against each other all the time. They kill each other over food, over a telephone, over a t.v. program, over a shower, over any and everything and it's 99% of

147

the time something very petty and inconsequential. We can see that another prisoner is hungry sometimes, and we won't even feed him, we won't care if he eats or not. That's the life of a prisoner, that's how we live in these places. Not caring anything at all about each other. We allow each other to die, without proper medical care, because the medical department doesn't care anything at all about us. They let us die without proper and adequate medical care all the time. We work in UNICOR, for 17 cents an hour, knowing that's not even enough to buy hygiene products for our bodies. We talk about each other negatively all the time rather than uplifting and helping each other. We hate to see each other progress and do positive things for ourselves. We don't self-check each other, we don't care what each other does to each other at all. All of these gangs in these Federal prisons, yet they are a pitiful sight to see, because they are 99% of the time, negative against each other. Their unity is within themselves and only to themselves. They are a negative force amongst themselves. Because they don't care about anyone but themselves they only care about each other and they usually only hurt, destroy, and self-destruct among each other. Because you never see them demanding or protesting non-violently about better conditions, or for reasonable good time, or for parole. All the gangs do is what gangs usually do, and that's stay to themselves and nothing positive.

The correctional officers kill us, murder us, assault us, write false reports against us, treat us like slaves, and indentured servants. Letting us die by not getting us to the hospital on time or denying us permission to even go to the medical department. The officers threaten us all the time with going to the special housing unit for 23-7, because they know we fear the lock downs. They know we are weak, they know we don't want to be in the cells 23-7. They know that we are separated without unity amongst each other. They know we despise and hate each other. They know all we do is rat and snitch on each other because we are weak. They know all they have to do is offer us some prison stamps, or a prison watch or radio, and we will rat and snitch on each other. The officers are trained and they go to training all the time in order to stay ahead and know what's going on with us prisoners. These correctional officers know a lot more about us, than we do about each other because they are trained to know for their own benefits, and for their own survival.

All we do is watch t.v., play cards, play sports, and do absolutely nothing positive for ourselves. In the meantime, the officers, the prison administration and the public is saying look at those darn fools in there. They don't want change for the better. Because all they do is murder, kill, assault, rape, and destroy and self-destruct against each other. They need to be where they are. The prison administration is not into allowing citizens into these Federal prisons on a regular basis. Because they really don't want the prisoners to get any rehabilitation unless they self-rehabilitate themselves on their own by themselves. The administration, honestly speaking, would rather see prisoners perish and decease before they lift a finger to help and assist prisoners. That just might be because they see exactly what I've been seeing and experiencing for the last 24 years in these Federal prisons. I honestly can't say I blame them, because we as prisoners are truly our own worst enemy to each other. We simply refuse to stand up for ourselves, and for positive and better change. We refuse to do what's right for and by each other. We are simply not only afraid of ourselves, but of each other as well. We simply stand for nothing at all and we go for any and everything. That is why we are as we are and treated as we are because we represent ourselves as nothing. It's true, we know this to be self evident, we know this to be true, and nothing but the truth.   I came from a world that was FREE and privileged paved with golden opportunities compared to the one from which I now exist in. Now I live in a confined world, a confined environment, with my conditions controlled and always monitored. Now, I have to philosophize, now I have to live a certain way or else I cannot live at all. Now, I have to possess a certain wisdom and live by that philosophy or even I will cease to exist within this world in which I now exist. Because this is no natural world, it's a vicious, unstable, schizophrenia world. Always changing back and forth, over and over, sideways, up and down, and sometimes all around. It's a world that needs positive and constructive change. But those prisoners that now exist in it, they don't care about positive and constructive change. All they care about is themselves individually, or gang wise, all they care about is negativity, murder, assault, stabbing and killing each other. All I care about is the law library and getting my FREEDOM one day, so that I can get as far away as I can from these rotten fools, who want nothing but negativity and a prison bed to sleep in because they refuse by choice, which is their own, to stand up for a better cause and for better change, so that upon their re-entry back into society, they will be a different and better individual than they were when they came here.

CHAPTER TWENTY-SEVEN

THE CROSS

The year is 2014, October. I sent another inmate back to court with the help and assistance of the Firm. We'll call him Bivens. He was a young, 24 year old Federal prisoner arrested for a major drug conspiracy in West Palm Beach, Florida. He was serving a 15 year sentence. He approached me in the prison unit where we both lived at one night around 8:30. I had just come from my daily routine in the law library. I came into the unit, approximately 130 something prisoners live in Unit B-2, in Coleman, Florida. I was walking to my cell when young Bivens approached me and asked me some legal questions. I answered briefly the legal questions he put to me, and told him I would get back to him. Several weeks later I did get back to him. I looked over all of his paper work and I told him that he had an ineffective assistance of counsel issue concerning the fact that counsel never appealed upon Bivens request of counsel to do so, and based on the excessive 15 year sentence, he was serving unconstitutionally. Because Bivens had not been responsible for the amount of drugs he had involuntarily, and unintelligently pled guilty to. His plea had therefore been an involuntary plea, based on an ineffective counsel, whom had not protected the defendant's Fifth, and Sixth Amendment rights and Rule 11 rights as well. I filed a Title 28 U.S.C. Section 2255 Motion for young Bivens. A few months later he was granted an Evidentiary Hearing, based on counsel's ineffectiveness and below the standard of representation. I provided young Bivens with mock hearings so that he would know exactly how to handle his situation truthfully and correctly without panicking like so many other prisoners do when they go to Court because all they like doing is watching t.v., playing sports, murdering and killing each other, so of course they won't know what to say when they go back to Court on an Evidentiary Hearing. And only very few of them will study their case period. This would turn out to be even a worse scenario than most of the other ones I sent back of 138 of them. Young Bivens encountered a guy in the Miami detention center by the name of Cowboy, a guy I knew from Coleman, but a guy young Bivens did not know. If you are a prisoner with a firm, like myself and As-Sadiq, with 138 wins and over 23 years in prison, then some of the other jail house pro-se litigants won't or usually don't like you, but won't accept the 24 years and let you go, and they can have the glory, the wins and everything else, just let me go. But they don't want that. They want to talk negative about you, fabricate about you, anything to assassinate your legal character, so that you don't lock the prison down with people bringing their cases to you. Typical prisoner jealousy in these prisons and typical prisoner assassination of another prisoner's character over jealousy. Cowboy asks young Bivens who did his case. Now Cowboy is serving a 15 year sentence, he's been incarcerated for about nine years on that 15 year sentence. I wonder damn, what is Cowboy doing in Miami Detention, when I just saw him last year right here in Coleman before he was transferred to Jessup FCI Medium in Jessup, Georgia. I ask young Bivens, are you talking about the Cowboy that was here? Young Bivens says yes! I say where do you know Cowboy from, he was not in Coleman when you were there. Young Bivens says, I met him in Miami Detention Center. And you let him see your legal work? Young

Bivens says yes! And he told young Bivens that I did not know what I was doing and that everything in the 2255 Motion I had filed for young Bivens was inaccurate. I said to young Bivens, Cowboy must be better than the government and the whole U.S. Attorney's Office. Because if they were not able to stop the Judge from giving you an Evidentiary Hearing on your issues, then how in the world can Cowboy be accurate about anything he told you? Young Bivens had allowed Cowboy to look over his legal work, not even knowing him first hand, rather than letting himself and his lawyer talk about his case first. Cowboy told young Bivens, what Stone did for you is all wrong, the Judge did you a favor by giving you that 180 months. Young Bivens goes into the Court room, and tells his lawyer and the Judge that he wants his Section 2255 Motion dismissed because Cowboy told him the 180 months was a favor from the Court. A young 24 year old African American male, no serious criminal history, no career offender, no Section 851 enhancement, and no serious criminal history, no career offender, and no armed career offender. Young Bivens gets his case dismissed, and does exactly what Cowboy told him. Cowboy then tells him he'll do it over for him for a fee. I did it for him for nothing, a favor will kill you faster than a bullet is the first thing that came to my mind. It's something my good friend As-Sadiq always told me. I looked at young Bivens and I said, it's on you pal!!!! And I walked away thinking to myself, damn!! These guys are crazy in this place. I said to myself, I wish I could have gotten that Evidentiary Hearing for myself, I would make legal history in that Court representing and explaining my case for my FREEDOM.

Time after time, prisoners do some of the craziest things when they appear in those Courts when I and the

Firm have sent them back to Court. But they will murder and kill and disrespect each other all day every day, and blame their problems on everybody else. But a lot of them refuse to stand up and stand firm for themselves for what is good and right for them. Whether they (prisoners) like what I am saying or not. It is simply the truth and nothing but the absolute truth. When I see young Bivens now, I simply say hello, pay my usual respects to the other prisoners and keep it moving. Because once I send them back, and they have counsel, whatever they do, it's on them from there on. My job is done once I win them an Evidentiary Hearing or a remand. Because I can't be in Court with them once I send them back. It's simply the nature of the business. And please whoever you are reading this book, please don't ever come to prison, because you will never be the same afterwards and that's for many different reasons. It's a place, like never before seen and or experienced and it will truly rock your world in many different ways.

CHAPTER TWENTY-EIGHT

CORRECTIONAL OFFICERS

99% of the officers think that guys in prison are the worst of the worst in society. The officers are trained to think that way. They are trained not to trust prisoners, don't believe anything they say, keep them at a distance of at least three feet. Keep your eyes on them at all times, read about at least one of them every 30 days, know who the high profile ones are. Learn what they say to each other, how they think, see what they are doing. Officers your security is always at stake being around these prisoners. Because they are here for committing crimes not only against you, but against society in general, against mankind and the world in general. The officers are trained to if they have to, murder you, assault you, in the event you breach any prison security, and/or become too aggressive with an officer. They are not supposed to harm, hurt, or assault you while in handcuffs, because you are already handcuffed, so no matter what you are saying, it means nothing because you are handcuffed, but a lot of officers will assault a prisoner while in handcuffs, knowing that prisoner cannot physically do anything to the officer. You have officers that put their jobs on the line or in jeopardy at times to help a prisoner, and that very same prisoner ratted and snitched on that officer. You have female officers that have liked a prisoner every now and then intimately, and that very same prisoner along with other rats and snitches told on that lady officer and got her fired from her job. And the prisoner's favorite words are Oh! She was a cop! That's a poor excuse to use, for telling on an officer who likes you or tried to help or assist you.

Someone like that is usually a rat, or snitch, or informer, or confidential informant from the very start. In other words, they were no good from the very start. And then you have those prisoners that rat on the officers, or civilians to try to get their sentence reduced. It's a damn shame, how prisoners will lie and rat on each other. So you as a civilian or an officer, definitely cannot trust them. And if you do, at least have the intelligence to look up under Title 18 U.S.C. Section 3553(f), Section 3553(e), U.S.S. Guideline 5K1.1, Criminal Procedure Rule 35(b). And then you'll know not to trust that prisoner at all. Now you have prisoners that were not rats before they came in, but now they become institutional or prison rats, and snitches. There is no way that if I was ever an officer, I would allow a prisoner to get too close to me personally without investigating him and finding out things about him, before I do anything for him. These prisoners today especially in the FEDS, are some rat, snitch, informing and confidential Mothers. If I were an officer in these penitentiaries, there is no way I would trust any Federal prisoner period, not one of them. Because you simply cannot trust them at all. You don't know them, nor anything about them, you don't know if they have rolled over and became a rat or snitch, or trying to compromise your job, your pension, your retirement. The prisoners don't care nothing about you, 99% of the time. Most of the time when an officer or civilian do end up trusting a prisoner, they usually trust one that was already a rat or snitch or was already that in his case, but that officer or civilian always seem to pick those type of prisoners to personalize themselves with. Because a prisoner that's not going to expose or tell or snitch on an officer is usually one not trying to communicate and/or have any contact with the officer or civilian because that prisoner doesn't want to be seen always talking to an officer or around an officer because it gives the prisoner a bad name always in an officer's or civilian's face. Real convict prisoners stay to themselves far away from officers and civilians and try to have as little contact with any officer or civilian as possible. Because he's usually a stand up type of guy and respected based on his principles as a prisoner convict, and he's usually not communicative at all with even his fellow prisoners. Those are the ones that <u>do</u> <u>not</u> <u>rat</u> or <u>snitch</u> <u>on</u> <u>any</u> <u>one</u>. Those are the ones that are usually very high profile, smooth, gangster types, and usually very sharp at their wits and will not tell or snitch on any one at all, ever, they will not rat or snitch, I guarantee my life on them, I've been here for 23 years I know. I've seen Federal prisoners rat on officers that were trying to help them, and those very same prisoners disappear off the compound and go testify against that officer. It's a damn shame. I've seen prisoners tell on female officers who like them, it's a damn shame. You would not believe it unless you were here to see it for yourself.

I see why a lot of those officers treat prisoners the way they treat them, and it's because we have no respect for ourselves, we don't self-check our own as we should, sometimes we do, 99% of the time we don't. I see why we are treated as we are, because that's how we conduct ourselves, and that's how we treat each other. Even when we were in control of some of the prisons when I first came to them, the officers gave us leeway, didn't harass us, didn't do a lot of things and all we did is disrespect each other, we self-destructed ourselves, and when we no longer had that control any more, all we did is what we are still doing to each other to this very day, and that is everything that I have already said in this book and that is disrespect each other and those that try to help and assist us. We as prisoners are completely disorganized, disenfranchised, dis-everything. We have no "Movement" among ourselves. We stand for nothing but destruction among each other. We are truly 95% of us afraid to stand up against each other, not the officers, not the civilians, but against each other and communicate to each other that those prisoners snitch, ratting, informing, confidential informants cannot live among us, cannot continue to be here, to destroy what we truly stand for. We have to self-check our own, not allow a dumb prisoner or stupid or retarded prisoner to turn a good officer bad because it shows we don't even check our own. We as prisoners need control among ourselves. That's why I say we don't have a movement among ourselves, to check each other when those checks need to be enforced. We do so much harm and hurt against even those who try to help and assist us. Even at the risk of some losing their jobs, we as prisoners still cross em, destroy their lives, knowing that ours is already in chaos and destruction mode, yet we allow it to happen and cause it to happen to someone trying to help and assist us.   What kind of prisoners are we, how did we ever get here with all this snitching, rating, informing, and confidential informing? Staff look at all of us and at what we are to ourselves, to the public, to the world, and to anyone that looks at the American Federal prison system.

I live in a world of confusion and yes constant disrespect, for anyone else that exists in it with me. But I live in it because I put myself in it, even when I did not have to, even when the Judges kept telling me I was headed the wrong way. Stop here Mr. Green, the right way is this way, not the way you are going. But like a damn fool, without a plan, without intelligence, I continued right on the path of no return, so here I am in the place of no return with 5 life terms plus 135 years, writing books, doing law work, hoping and praying that one day, I just might find my way out and go the way those Judges told me for so long, and for so many years, Mr. Green, this is not the right way, it's here, over there. But they became tired and discontent and rightfully so with my constant ignorance and stupidity and said one day if this is the road and path that you insist on traveling, then so let it be, and because we have told you, Mr. Green, so many times in the past that it was not the road to travel because of what was in front of it and where it would lead you, but because you insisted on traveling it any way, here is five life terms, and a Ball 135 for you. Damn Fool!!! And that I was, but now I see the light and it is never too late for one to rehabilitate himself. Never! And that I truly did over the years with the help of so many others that I encountered along the other way of traveling who had also traveled that very same road, and journeyed that very same path that I had. Some have since left and/or departed, and some never will and they know this to be a fact. But I, myself, have to keep trying because I don't believe in giving up and I never will. But I now travel a totally different road, but this one is so much better and realistic then the one that I caused myself 5 life terms plus a Ball 135.

CHAPTER TWENTY-NINE

PRISON LIFE IN GENERAL

One never knows what it is to hate, until he comes to prison. Because it seems to be one of the things prisoners do when they come to prison. They hate against each other. They learn how to hate against each other. And when they leave these prisons, they have already become haters, because they hate to see each other doing good or something constructive. These prisons are where you see fear, hate, aggressiveness, and brutality. These are the places where it is produced and distributed at. These are the people that prisons produce and manufacture back to the American public. This is part of the prison education one receives before his reentry back into society.

The prison Administration stays keeping inmates in fear with lock downs, constant misbehavior retorts, aggressive attitudes towards inmates, unnecessarily. Staring inmates down, looking and treating inmates as if they are the scum of the earth, or slaves on a plantation. Inmates in return, stare them down, challenge them mentally, physically, and any other way they deem appropriate in order to get their point back across that they are not who the Administration is projecting them to be. It's a constant standoff at times.

The prison cells are tactics; if you are not conforming to the prison rules, you will never come out of these cells, you will stay lonely, something most prisoners cannot seem to accept and Master "Loneliness", being by themselves for long periods of time without human contact in these places. The prison Administration knows this and uses it constantly to their

160

advantage against the prisoners, by constantly locking them up and serving them misbehavior reports for any little fiction. Lock em up, put him in the Special Housing Unit (HOLE), which is a cell, by yourself, for 23 hours a day for as long as they deem appropriate, and/or the misbehavior reports sanctions you to be confined. The prison Administration makes it their business to control inmates through fear, hollering at them, "Lock it down!" Right now! This is an institution lock down, go immediately to your cells," as loud as they can holler. And it works 99.9% of the time too. Now, remember, these are inmates that were gangsters on the streets, crocks, thugs, murders, robbers, con men, extortionists, crime bosses, gang leaders, you name it, they are here. The government knows exactly how to keep them in fear. All they do is hate on each other, talk about each other, hate to see each other with something they don't have. They are constantly telling on each other all the time, and getting each other killed and murdered, and stabbed, and hating each other because of the color of their skin. You would not believe this mess, you would have to see it to believe it. And I must say as well, when inmates leave these places, they are usually more intelligent, but bitter, I mean more intelligent in the criminal sense in our world of crime, because that's all we talk about in these places 24 hours a day is crime. You become more dangerous and vicious in these places, you learn not to care about anybody or anything. These prisons make you like that, they turn you into a cold blooded killer, and you become brutal in these places and very serious in order to survive if you are to return back to society. You do what you have to do in order to make it out of these places alive.

Despair and Loneliness are always with you in

these places, life is very empty in these places, with nothing to do. You have to create things to do if you expect to come out of these places with a rational mind. I stay constantly in the law library on the computers, because the Administration has taken all of the law books away, and we only have access to computers now. The law library is my life, every day, six days a week, I'm in it, and when I get headaches from being in there so much, I relax for a few days and come right back to researching doing cases along with other cases that I am doing.

In prison you will eventually learn that it is not worth breaking the law, and giving up your "FREEDOM" for this type of life. You'll eventually say one day to yourself, "damn this ain't it, this ain't what I signed up for." This is crazy. Yea! The whole environment and atmosphere is crazy.

You become like your fellow prisoners in these places, you can't avoid it. I haven't seen one that hasn't as of my 23 years in being in here myself. The Administration in these places are not going to help and assist prisoners in becoming better and productive members of society, because if they did, they would be out of a job!! But a lot of prisoners are proud of their criminal endeavors and wouldn't change, nor disregard or be embarrassed about what they have done, and what they represent in life, because they feel this is who they are, what they have always longed to be.

Prison is a part of what goes along with the consequences one faces once he is arrested for whatever crime he commits. It is up to the prisoner how he does his sentence, whether it is easy or good time, bad or rough, it's on him. He's the one doing the time. Remember that saying about "mind your business and if you don't bother anyone they won't bother you? That is totally false in prison. The ones minding their own business trying to stay out of trouble are always the ones having problems. That's usually because they are trying to avoid problems and conflicts in a very vicious and hostile environment, that is saturated with murders, killings, stabbings, rapes, and conflicts all the time, especially when you are trying to avoid this.   It's as if it comes right to you and tests you for your strength or weaknesses, it takes your virility if you are not strong and makes you weak it you don't enforce whatever penalty that you must on that individual for the problem he caused you, revenge, 90% of the time in these places is a must if another prisoner has wronged or disrespected you. What I mean by disrespected is looked at you in a certain way, walked by you in a certain way, gave you a certain impression, took something from you, or stole something from you, bumped into you without saying excuse me, interrupted into your conversation with another inmate and did not say excuse me. Those are some of the wrongs and disrespect that an inmate will usually immediately respond to, especially calling you out by name, and or saying something about you that cannot be verified. Those are wrongs and disrespects that inmates consider worthy of revenge or immediate responses to.

When these guys are released out of these places, a lot of them never rebuild their personality or develop new social values, or constructive or positive characters. If the system demanded change in convicts like rebuilding of their personalities, social values, a lot of correctional officers would not have jobs. Because a lot of these guys would never return back to prison. Because prisoners would have developed new and better attitudes about themselves and toward society in general. The system robs them of their humanity because their Freedom is so restricted. They live in a world of constant violence, drama, and conflict. Their personalities usually stay that way even when they are released for some time unless they chose to make change on their own. But they never forget where they came from and who they became and how they changed from a world of Freedom into a world of murder, stabbings, and constant conflict. It is not something that just goes away once you are released from prison.

No matter who you were on the streets, it means something, but you still have to prove yourself all over again, once you enter into these prisons. Like I said, you have all kinds of people in the FEDS from all over the world. Everybody seems to have been somebody and nobody wants to be a nobody. So there is constant personality conflicts, whether they be physical, mental, or spiritual, crime bosses who were bosses on the streets, but in here they are usually low profile, because they know the system will lock em down 24 hours, 7 days a week for any little mishap. Remember now, there are gangsters here, real ones, there are killers and murderers here, real ones, there are all kinds and types all bunched in together, 1700 in this joint. If you are not extremely careful, you will cease to exist in these places. The system intentionally creates this kind of chaos because you have them all together, with hardly no programs, nothing to do, but stab, murder, assault and kill each other. They're cancelling each other out like damn fools. They just don't seem to see until 5 or ten years later, when that 20 or 30 years they had is now 2 or three life terms. It's a damn shame how the system promotes such chaos, and they prosecute these guys, and keep them forever.

Thereby, always having a security blanket for a job, in the FEDS. There is no college in these prisons I'm traveling to, there is no real or serious programs in these joints I'm traveling to, the Federal Bureau of Prisons took 99% of them away and the U.S. Senate took the college programs because the public did not want prisoners educating themselves and going to college when they said they couldn't send some of their own kids to college, so why should inmates be able to go. That is why there are no more colleges in the prisons I've been to.

There is too much violence in these prisons. There is too many illiterate inmates in these prisons that need immediate educations for their own mental health and safety. There is hardly any programs in these places period. The prisons are over populated with some of them with three inmates in a cell. It's getting worse and worse all the time. If this continues on the path that it's on, it's going to explode and it's going to be not just bad, but extremely terrible. I see another Attica, another New Mexico, another Lucasville, another SoleDad. But it can be prevented with an immediate injection of population decrease, more and much better educational programs, and better law libraries. It's that simple, but the average Federal Bureau of Prison employee reading this book will probably say, we don't need to do any of these things, we've got these inmates under control. But that's the same thing they said about Attica, Lucasville, Ohio, and New Mexico, until they blew up. Hopefully the FEDS will and already has seen it before it happens. Because the warning signs are there. The hand writing is on the wall. But knowing the FEDS like I've come to know them, and learn what I have learned from this system, once they see it clearly as I do, they will usually do something about it, before it gets to deep, or out of control. Then again maybe they won't because sometimes even they (government) get the impression that it won't happen, like with the crack cocaine riots. It's a vicious cycle in this system. If you are not careful it will swallow you up and you too will never see the light of day. I know because I've seen it happen on several occasions since my incarceration.

When you are in these prisons, and you are in here for a while, you come to realize that all the Wardens know is NO! To this, NO! To that, NO! 99% of the time it's NO to whatever you reasonably ask them for, such as for better law libraries, better educational programs, better living conditions, better medical. These people look at you as if you are a slave, you are getting nothing 99% of the time. They (government) will murder you too, and cover it up as if it was an accident. As I've said they talk to you like you are a slave, they treat you like a slave, they don't care nothing about you, but the few I've named to you already. They were intelligent and reasonable. And, when the correctional officers are trained, or come from training, the government trained them to hate inmates, to despise inmates, to treat them like slaves, like they are nothing with absolutely no rights at all. Don't trust those inmates, keep em three feet away from you, here is a profile on Sly Green, he's this, he was arrested for this. He's presently doing this and that. We are hearing this and that about Sly Green. They train those officers to hate everything about an inmate and they tell em, he's a killer, he's a murder, he's a King pin, he's this, he's that. Now as if that's not bad enough, some inmates are so illiterate, not all of them, but a lot of them, they tell the correctional officers and the Administration everything that's going on in the prison just like in the slavery days. You wouldn't believe what goes on in these Federal and State prisons. These very same inmates being oppressed are helping the Administration oppress themselves. The correctional officers have inmates terrorized in fear, this is because they see what inmates do to each other. And they say those guys won't stand firm on nothing, they won't agree on the weather forecast. They are so disorganized and discombobulated, it's a damn shame.

You have correctional officers who have tried to help inmates in whatever way they could, but 99% of those inmates go right to the Administration and snitch on that very officer that tried to help and assist him.

It's a damn shame. Then that very inmate says to the other inmates, oh! They the police, but that same police was helping you and you ruined his life and told on him for a time cut off of your sentence. Rats, snitches, and informers. It's straight crazy in these places. Most of the things that happen with the inmates, they usually bring it on themselves. 99% of the time, they do it to themselves and blame it on the Administration and say they are at fault because we are in here killing each other over a t.v., a telephone, or an E-Mail, and how we look at each other. Paranoia, schizophrenia personalities. It's crazy, and it's insane too, and like I've said throughout the book: You have to be extremely careful in these places or you could easily lose your life.

I remember one day, I was in Schyulkill, Pennsylvania, an FCI joint. I was on a ten minute break outside the law library. When I would go out on the break, I would always see this guy, standing outside on the break as well. But I would not say anything to him, I had been incarcerated for about 13 years, so I knew when to speak and when not to speak. One Saturday on the break in the morning time, the guy asks me my name and I said it's Stone. He asks me where I was from and I said Buffalo. Then he asks me how long have I been incarcerated and I told him 13 years and some change. Then he asks what I was in jail for and I said RICO Enterprise, 848, drug charges, conspiracy, etc. Then he tells me his name is Horse, and he's from Cincinnati, Ohio and he has been in for 26 years, and that I reminded him of a guy that had been in another Federal prison that was in the State of Washington that the FEDS had closed down in the eighties. It was a prison on the water, Horse said that the guy stayed going to the law library every day and working and working on his case for about 22 years, and one day he got his Freedom. Horse said don't worry yourself, Stone, you'll get back one day. You work too hard not to, so just stay focused and stay at it and you'll win it eventually. You will win something because you are trying and nothing beats a failure but a try, because at least you are trying. Horse said, "I'm going to start dropping jewels on you every once and a while," and then he dropped the first one on me. He said one day there was this guy he was in Marion, Illinois, the worst Federal prison since Alcatraz. The guy had murdered two people and they were at recreation in the Rec. cages and he asked the guy why did he murder those two inmates, and the guy walking back and forth in the cages stopped suddenly and looked at him, and said Horse it was all just a misunderstanding. Mr. Horse, told me, never leave a situation without making sure everything is settled before walking away from it. Always settle or take care of it as fast as possible or handle what needs to be handled, so that there not be or continue to be a misunderstanding. Because a misunderstanding not settled can keep you incarcerated for the rest of your life.

So try not to have misunderstandings with anyone at all. I said to Mr. Horse, YO! Horse, give me another one of those jewels, and he said, NO! Not right now, I'll give them slowly, be patient young Stone. I'll drop em as we go. From then on for as long as Mr. Horse was there at Schyulkill, I watched and waited for our 10 minute breaks, hoping he would drop one of those jewels, and slowly with patience, he dropped a lot of them on me. I learned a lot from Mr. Horse, until he left. I was grateful to God for sending him my way. Because today I live by those jewels that he constantly dropped on me until he was transferred to another prison. As I went on, I would learn and comprehend many more things and always trying to relate them to my Freedom. Every and anything was about Freedom to me. That's why I avoided a lot of things, that's why I'm not dead in here, or wounded, or any of that nonsense. FREEDOM FREEDOM Family!!

CHAPTER THIRTY

THE LAW CLASSES

After teaching the law classes for a few years, I gave it to As-Sadiq, along with Young Magnum, as his assistant. I honestly felt that As-Sadiq would be a better teacher than myself because he has so much to offer in the law to the class. I also gave him the recommendation to be the head of the Firm. Because I felt that he had so much more to offer us all, so I relinquished that position to him as well. Everything now comes through him, and hopefully Young Magnum, might one day lead if he's not free by then. I'm presently as always focusing on new issues for my case, and trying to find a win in my research or through the research of one of the researchers in the Firm. It feels great to know that we can depend on each other in the Firm and believe in each other as well. But again my mind goes back and forth to what I have to constantly deal with in these places from day to day and you would be surprised on how crazy things can get, how fast one can lose his life over nothing. But this is the price we pay for being in a place like this, or any of these Federal prisons. I have to inform you that if you stay too long in these places, you can lose feelings for things you once felt sorry for or about especially when you see someone in pain or hurting or complaining about something. Because these places are always forcing you mentally to be strong and don't show weakness or concern for the next individual or anything like that. Be strong, stand up, stay focused, be firm at all times. These places are always saying let the weak suffer, intimidate the weak, take advantage of the weak, crush em, destroy em, that's why they say these places are no places for the timid or the weak. I live in a world where only the strong survive, and sometimes not even all them because they get to thinking they are too strong and someone else comes along and shows them just how strong they are. I am around 1700 inmates every single day, I know them like reading a book. Imagine being around thousands of convicts for 23 years of your life, that's definitely a psychology issue if I have ever seen one. Because I can tell you almost anything about men especially if they are weak or strong or whatever! I know them, I live among all kinds of them from all over the world. In these places, who would ever think I would be doing a case for a doctor, or a lawyer, or a drug lord, for gangsters, con men, hustlers, stickup boys, fraud guys, thieves, killers, murders and rich guys, if you only knew, because I do. I sit back sometimes and I think about what I could have done with my life and how I came to be who I became and why. I think of my family and how being in here I lost a lot of them to the streets and to life in general. I think of how I lost my Moms, my Father, my brother and sister, and how good my other sister has always been to me that I call every day or as much as I can. I think of how I could have been so much better to my daughter and two sons, and how I miserably failed them by being in here most of my life. I think of how good they made it without me though and how much I love them. I'm always thinking, it's something I love doing. I think of the guys that went crazy, because they couldn't do the time they were given, and I say to myself I ain't going out like that because I'm not getting weak for nobody, I don't care if I die in this place, I'm not going crazy, the law won't allow that because I'm doing something I like and that's law. It's never ending, and you can't nail it down because it's always changing and I'm always there looking at the change in case it's a change for my freedom.

I think about at times how I first went to Leavenworth, Kansas United States Penitentiary, I said to myself damn! This place is like a killing field. United States Penitentiary at Lewisburg, was the same and so was that vicious joint at Florence High Security Colorado. They were all very treacherous, and yet United States penitentiary Atlanta, it was cool and yes very dangerous, but not worth doing time at a place like that as well. I simply hated them all because of the constant danger they posed to my Freedom. Because too much comes with it, in the stay. If you are not careful you'll definitely cease to exist. I think about how I made it through all of these penitentiaries and how I got to where I am now. I've always said and admitted to myself that I'm standing to the death. It will be the only thing that takes me down because I'm not tolerating anything but the real.

I think about how far advanced in my thinking from what I once was and how I was perceived when I was free. I wonder and wonder in my thinking of what would have been had I still been free, and then I think back to where I am and wonder if I'll ever get back regardless of how hard I try to.

I walk the prison yard, usually by myself thinking of this and that, because I have forever to think about everything. When I'm exercising I'm thinking. Prison is a place for thinking because I find myself doing it constantly. I think and wonder about my friends and the ones that deceased while I've been here. I think about the ones that testified against me, and the ones that fabricated against me. I think of how the government called special Assistant U.S. Attorneys in from

Washington to help prosecute me, including the ones that were already there from Buffalo. I think about how they (government) used their security alone to help them win their case against me. How they don't care how they take you down, whether it's true or not they don't care. If they want you off the streets they simply will do any and everything to win. The government is in the game of winning and that is what they do and that is by any means necessary. That is why 97% of the Federal prisoners plead guilty. Because they are afraid of the government. The government puts them in fear and extorts them into believing that if they don't plead guilty they are going to put them away for as long as possible, if not forever. The average prisoner went for that, regardless if he was innocent or not. That fear, the extortion by the government forced that prisoner not to go to trial. Instead like a damn fool, he/she pled guilty and got 15, 20, 30, years or a life sentence after being enhanced multi-times under unconstitutional guidelines that violated that very prisoner's Fifth, Sixth, and Eighth Amendment rights to due process, to a jury determination beyond a reasonable doubt, and to cruel and unusual punishment to a draconian and very severe sentence. Here are 1700 inmates in this prison and don't you know, not even 50 of them will participate in our law classes, that As-Sadiq teaches and Young Magnum assists in teaching. These guys in prison won't even try to educate themselves on a mass level.   Some do, but the mass majority won't and don't care, and won't even try. Yet, they want rights, and privileges and opportunities to be better citizens upon reentry back into society. This is madness and you would never believe it unless you see it. I think about these things, but I can't go out on a limb for them, because most of them will say

I'm crazy, they'll expose my sincere assistance to them from my heart for them to the Administration. They will isolate me in Colorado for the rest of my entire sentence. I never want to see Colorado again unless it's something worth seeing it for. Not for some inmates telling on me to the Administration for trying to help them better themselves and looking like a dam fool for helping them locked down in Colorado. A place I've never liked when I was there over 15 years ago.

CHAPTER THIRTY-ONE

THE D.C. MOB, AND OTHER STATE MOBS

Before I touched down in the federal system, I was always hearing about Washington DC the Mob from guys that had already been to the FEDS. I would hear crazy things such as a lot about homosexuality, extortion, murder, assaults, everything negative. But, when I got into the FEDS they were not the vicious guys I had heard about or don't appear to be. They were real cool African American guys. They were for their people like any other race. And I got along with them very well. They control the Federal system. They ARE the Federal system. They are very loyal to each other. They stick together, they roll together, they do everything together and yes, they truly are the REAL DEAL to the very end. In the FEDS they are loyal and powerful, to each other. I say the D.C. Mob, because they are organized. They move out seriously when they have to, and they are not cowards, nor lames, nor chumps. They are like a Black Mafia in the FEDS.

A lot of other states in the FEDS fear the D.C. Mob. They should because those guys don't come to play at all! Mr. Linnwood Gray, Big Koola (Freeman), Tony Hamlin, Young Tone, Spoon, O.G. Butch Woods, Wooten Bey, Nelson Bey, Mr. Coleman Bey, Mr. Abornathy Bey, (The General) and many others from that Mob. These guys were some of the Shot Callers from D.C. and they meant business too. Having seen nearly nor hardly any of the negative things I was told about the D.C. Mob, my opinion of them is positive and a lot of guys from other states hang tough with the D.C. Mob; they too like and respect them like they should or would any other Mob in the FEDS. One of the best guys I ever encountered from the D.C. Mob, was Big Koola (Freeman), Tony Hamilton, P-Life, Spoon, Butch Woods, and especially Mr. Linnwood Gray. I love and respect those guys because they are the REAL DEAL. They keep it "Frosty"!!

THE CALIFORNIA MOB

The California Mob is cool too. Big Tweet, Big Bud from Hoover, T.J. Benzo Ed, Sin Bad, Big Bones (Woodard), Nuke, Tray Kay, Slick, Doc Holliday, Truck, and many others. They were all very cool, and they were from the Cal. Mob in California. Both Bloods and Crips, and they truly represented that too.

THE CHICAGO MOB

Peewee, Ready Red, G-Money, Big "D", Big Perry, Milk, Marco Thomas, and many others, they too were cool and real.

THE NEW YORK MOB

Big Jerry Rahem from Queens (Boston), Big Con from the Bronx (Diaz), Walter Cook (Ice), Bob Lemon (The Boxer), GEO from the Bronx, Spanish Steve from the Bronx, (Ronnie Bump and "Supreme" are in a class of their own), and I did not forget you Guy Fisher. Rahem from Brooklyn, Sha from Harlem, Cyrus Benning and Rashid Austin, both from Buffalo, As-Sadiq, and A.I., Yaw-Yaw from Harlem, Big Scoop from Yonkers, (The Young General, "For Real"), Shabazz (Bustic), Born Allah, Shakim Allah, and yes Dakim from

Buffalo, and the Bronx, Nay-Nay from Brooklyn. All of them were real and yes, Dapper Dan too. They truly represent that New York State of gangster mind set. And I did not forget you Prince and C-Just, and Tucker, and Bing. And I would never ever forget my good friends Tu-Quam, and Gotti Johnson, and definitely not Big King from Mount Vernon. They were all very real and cool and "Beaver" up and coming and always keeping it real.

THE PHILLY MOB

Tyrik (Loranzu Ducam), T.L. (Tony Long), Kubini Savage, Reggie 6-9, Big A1, and many others from Philly were cool.

THE DETROIT MOB.

Omar Kill a Regg, Slim Bo, Big Monn (Bentley), they were real to the death.

THE CONNECTICUT MOB.

Big G (Morales), No-El, Big Twin, Slim, they were the truth.

THE FLORIDA MOB.

John-John, Blood Hound, Bo-Didly, Yuk, Big Scoop, Eddie-Bo, Young Yogi, Theo, Bullock, Money Clip, Longly, B&G, Big E, Big Seven, Pee-Zo, TomTom, Dickey, Big Champ, Big Bub, Young Magnum, J.C. Charlie, the Ford Brothers, the Lee Brothers, Corn Head, and I did not forget you Gangster Curt,

Hollywood, Rich Mike Delaney, GoonBay and Big Seven. They were all cool and represented their state as required. But Bomba, the General of all Generals out of Florida, a Cuban mobster, seriously represented the Spanish mob from the South and it also appears to be everywhere he goes, they come to him from all races and colors, it's something I've never seen until I encountered Bomba from Miami, Florida, and he was so much more than just Florida, he is truly world wide with his gangster and Gentleman respect. I'm just calling it like I know it and like I see and saw it.

This Federal prison system is, and can be, straight crazy and at times totally out of control. This is the world I live in, it is the world from which I study, it is the world from which I am trying so hard to never ever see and or ever have to experience again. But I'm labeled now in my own city, and therefore, it's extra hard for me, because of what the government built a picture of me into the minds of my fellow Americans in the city from which I came, which is Buffalo, New York. But I have to keep trying to win, and FREE myself. I can never ever stop trying for my FREEDOM. It's why I live in the law library every day, I have to go, I have to research, I have to try to get myself FREE. Because I do not like nor appreciate the life I gave myself, nor how I put myself in the situations I did. Again and again I tell you, no one but me is the blame for what has transpired with me, but me.   And now I must fight to the death, or to FREEDOM or else as I have already told you, I too will decease in a Federal United States penitentiary, never ever seeing society ever again. So I try and I try, and I try, again, and again, until I can't again or I succeed or decease trying. But until then, I live in a world littered with chaos, confusion, constant difficulties, and mad men, mad at you, mad at the world, mad at me too, and/or anyone else who refuses to hear their story and/or adhere to their madness and I do mean madness too!!!

For those of you who read this book, I sincerely need you to understand or at least try to comprehend, that this world of mine from which I write this book. It's a world unlike other worlds you would have ever encountered. I promise you, if you were to enter this world, not only would you never ever be the same ever again from just your experiences in my world, but you would rather live on Mars where you think they just might have life, than to risk living in my world. Because in mine all they do is take each other's lives, ruin each other's lives, tell on each other, lie on each other, steal from each other, rape each other, stab each other, disrespect each other, speak negative of each other, set each other up, hit each other over a t.v., fight over a telephone, kill over a t.v. that is not even theirs, murder or assault you over a phone call, tear up and destroy everything they touch and then complain for more. The world I live in, they don't care how they are treated. They like being treated the way they are because they do it to themselves, they refuse to stand firm and together for a change in the system. They don't care how the administration talks to them or do what they do to them. They must not, because they never stand up against it. If the administration takes the phones and t.v.'s and the recreation and their lives, you know what they would say? OH!! I don't watch t.v. anyway, I don't go to recreation anyway, that's their excuse for not being firm and standing up for change. Most of them are already serving 15, 20, 30 years, life and multi-life for little or no drugs. Yet day after day they hurt and disrespect each other, day after day refuse change, they are me and I am they, but they refuse FREEDOM and positive change in a system cluttered with disrespect and diseased minds that respect nothing but negativity, and disrespect for each other. I come from this world, I live in it still right now. You tell me, why on earth would you ever choose to live next door in cell 5, with me? Why would you even, knowing what I just told you is a 100% the truth, and nothing but the truth.

Every day, I see all the Mobs, every day, I walk past and I speak to those who speak to me and or respect me as I do them. And every day, I pray, and sometimes I pray for others as I do for myself. Every day, I dream from within the world I am for FREEDOM. Because now I see the way, now I see light, and now just might be too late. But I keep trying until I can't any more or until they say Green pack it up, you are out of here. You finally made it. Or they might just say one day, the guy you all once knew as Sly Green, is no more, he's gone into another atmosphere never ever to be seen again.

All I know is that I have to stay focused and keep trying because Hope, Prayers, and God is all I have going for me now. Everybody else is either gone or turned their backs on Sly Green, with the exception of a very few. But it's neither here nor there, because in order for me to win I must fight and fight, and fight until!!!!

CHAPTER THIRTY-TWO

I BECAME WHO I AM

Trapped, caught, busted by the FEDS, and the State of New York, Buffalo, the home from which I came. Alone but not anxious for any company. Always thinking, sometimes dangerously, about the past. Not broke, and never bending, but unable to pull the chains of prison from around my Federal Penitentiary neck. Mentally stable, spiritually endured, and educationally. Always searching for legal issues of FREEDOM. Knowing that they told me, I'd never ever see the streets again. Not convinced, but know it's a reality if I do not win. Therefore, I stay focused, ready for whatever and always on point, because if I am not, then I'll lose my own life usually over something foolish and petty – what else can a prisoner lose his life for in these places, but for something usually negative, none valued especially when it's weighed against the odds of FREEDOM. Everybody seems to have flipped on you because you are incarcerated, many not wanting to have anything at all to do with you. Everybody slides away, all of them gone. By yourself, not caring after some years, but always wondering and asking yourself why? But never knowing that good guys always come in last.

Being mentally stronger in these places, spiritually and mentally, but a 1,000 more times dangerous than you ever were. But that's because of the environment you are in. The condition in prison you are subjected to, and the spirit of the joint, is always murder, kill, stab, assault, and you must not fail for if you do, then you too become just another victim. It happens all the time. Gangs, groups, bosses, leaders, followers, they are all here. All of them, just about, want legal questions answered. New jail house lawyers you can count them on your hand, that's how extinct they are. Needed Yes! They are! God! To the prison population. Yes! Usually highly protected from danger, but not if they blow a certain case, even though they can't win them all, one loss can cost them their life, or an assault upon them. Crime the story of the day, always every day. That's all we know, that's all we want, it's all we see, and glorify. There's not too much of anything else to do, but that. Because many of us don't see the forest for the trees. Ignorance, stupidity, impulse, murder, assault, is always on the menu, for every meal you desire. Educational progress, programs, law library, books, reading, anything positive and constructive of that nature is hard to find on the menu of the day. Because they are usually out of those items.

I came into this prison world learning a prison philosophy. Mastering it, and creating my own as I serve my own sentence. Looking at my peers, watching what they do, listening to what they say, building later on what they said, what I heard, and what I learned from being incarcerated for so very long. Creating my own prison philosophy along the way.

Reading became a must. George Jackson, Jack Henry Abbot, Gary Gilmore, James Carr, Malcolm X, Martin Luther King, Jr., Machiavelli, 48 Laws of Power, The Art of Seduction, 33 Degrees of War, African and American History, all the philosophy I can read on Socrates, Plato, Aristotle, Thales of Miletus, Salon of Athens, The pharaohs of Egypt, Law Books, Religion, and anything else that had any kind of intelligence to it and meaning.

Observation of my fellow prisoners, I watched

everything they did for the last fifteen years and more. To the point that I am able to just about predict what they will and what they won't say and do in these places. I became a master at reading body language in these places. Especially about when and how my fellow prisoners move when they are about to have physical, spiritual and mental drama with each other.

I became a master at observing why all they do is watch t.v., play cards all day, play chess all day, play sports every day all day.

I observed the mess hall to the extent that if I saw the slightest sign of this or that I knew exactly what to do and how to move immediately.

I mastered why we go to religious services all the time, and stay in the churches as much as we do in these places.

I always know who is around me, what's in my environment, and what's always going on around me as much as possible. That's a must.

I always keep certain prisoners from getting too close to me or around me, depending on who they are and what they are in prison for because my philosophy taught me to be extremely careful about that because it could cost me my own life.

I simply came up with my own philosophy after being incarcerated for so long, I clearly mastered my environment. The more I learned, the more I realized how I had ruined my own life. The more I learned, I realized that you become a danger to many of your own fellow prisoners. Why? because like I said! All 90% of them do is play sports, play cards, watch t.v.. They do all the things they should not be doing. They do them because they say they have nothing else to do. They say it passes the time away. But what about education, what about school, what about college, what about programming, what about reading books, getting their G.E.D., striving to better their position in life. YES! What about if they say, they simply don't care. 99% of them don't care and would never ever go to war or non-violently stand up for college, better medical, good time, parole, and respect for their manhood. YES! They'll murder, kill, stab, take advantage of each other and sacrifice each other to the prison administration for a book of stamps, institutional stamps at that. But I figured it all out as I went on to create my own prison philosophy.

I now know what it is. It's fear of the administration, it's fear of being locked down for months at a time, it's fear of standing up for something positive that will help them, rather than ruin them. My philosophy tells me, that my fellow prisoners are afraid of change and therefore, refuse to stand up for it. They don't believe they can acquire it, they don't want to suffer the consequences for it. They don't see it. And they will never ever see it because they are afraid of the consequences behind accomplishing it. And therefore, they will say and do anything to avoid change and stop it from happening. My 24 years of philosophy tells me this, it's been proven to me time in and time again, based on my physical observations and the results of these physical observations. We will never see change for the positive if we do not stand up together for it. We will always be the scum of the earth, slaves, misfits, a menace to society, indentured servants, the lowest of the lowest. And it will always be because we do not respect ourselves. We do not self-check each other when we know we are wrong and what that wrong can bring. We have no substance to our madness, we even rape, assault, and kill our own mentally ill prisoners. We steal from them and laugh at them when we know they need us, when we know we are all in here together. Yet, we still don't care anything about each other. My philosophy tells me after all these years of being incarcerated, that no matter how I try to get my fellow prisoners to want to change, they never will until they are one day forced to see what some of us already see, but still fail to effect change amongst the masses of us all. And until we do, we will always be as I say afraid of our own shadow, and continue to be looked at all over the world as "nothing". My philosophy tells me that...

CHAPTER THIRTY-THREE

SHOT CALLERS

The shot callers are not usually respected or in that position because of how intelligent they are. They are usually shot callers in that position because they are extremely dangerous physically when necessary, which is most of the time. You hardly ever see a convict who's a shot caller that's very intelligent. Most of them that are, can hardly think of how to get across the street, because if they had to a car would knock most of them to their knees, because they wouldn't know how to think to cross the street. That's how unintelligent most of them are. They (convicts) would rather take advantage of the intelligent convict, and disrespect him because he's always thinking, he's always thinking of something constructive and positive. Something that's going to help Free him, something that will help make life better for him while he's incarcerated, something educational, for a better future. Convicts don't want those type of guys usually to be their shot callers. Because they think too good and too much, and too positive. Convicts want a shot caller whose extremely physical and violent, one that's personality is intensely violent. A guy that will go on impulse. It's a damn shame how convicts, the mass majority of them, don't want to do anything to better themselves. All they do is watch t.v., play cards, play sports, watch sports, fight, stab, injure, talk about each other, murder and kill each other, for little or nothing. They become intensely violent in these places. Their personalities become conflicted with violence on a constant basis. These prisons affect their lives basically for the rest of their lives if they don't try to change for the positive, which most of them don't want to do. Plain and simple, it's a pitiful episode in these places.

My fellow prisoners ignite violence against each other over the stupid things. They murder, assault and disrespect each other over who was next on the phone, why did you change it to that channel, why are you looking at me like that, I don't like how you walked across my path. You simply would not believe the illiteracy, the ignorance, and the notorious and vicious feuds convicts have with each other over something that's usually about nothing. They seem to love taking advantage of each other physically and with mental games. They constantly disrespect each other. You remember the saying "don't kill the messenger?" Well these guys, they kill the messenger and they always want you to do something for them, before they do something for themselves. It's amazing how they have education classes, and the mass majority of them refuse to get their G.E.D. or even try to take outside college courses. They'll use any excuse not to help themselves. They don't have a lot of programs in these Federal prisons at all. They should have college programs taught inside these Federal prisons, so that guys can get their degrees, and learn how to be better and more productive citizens, but even the system is flawed and corrupt, because they don't seem to care with the exception of Wardens, Mr. Holt, and his brother, Mr. Mickey Ray, and Mr. Scott Didrull and a few other Wardens. The convicts won't stand up for better anything unless it's for drugs or murder, or assault or talking about each other. But they involuntarily stay locked down for months at a time for something stupid and dumb. But not for better educational purposes, not for parole, or for better computers, or for anything positive. When I first came into the Federal system, over 20 years ago, some convicts were actually in control of various Federal Prisons. But the Administration took em back, because all the convicts did was assault each other, disrespect each other, kill each other, and do primative things to each other. They simply won't do what is right and best for each other as a whole. It's a dam shame and that's why we are treated the way we are. The convicts want to blame everything on the Administration but it's not the Administration 99% of the time. It's "us", it's our own fault, it's our own mistakes, we just simply refuse to accept that, and have to have someone to blame for what we do to each other.

CHAPTER THIRTY-FOUR

THE FEDERAL SYSTEM
AS I KNOW IT
AND
AS I SEE IT THROUGH MY EYES

I minced no words when I said that United States Federal Penitentiaries such as Leavenworth, Kansas, Florence, Colorado, Lewisburg, Pennsylvania, and USP Atlanta, Georgia were the most dangerous Federal prisons I have ever experienced. It was war all the time in those penitentiaries, with inmates fighting inmates, inmates constantly murdering and killing each other, just because of the color of their skin. Inmates, constantly ridiculing each other because of some reason or another. We inmates never stand together for positive things, such as better educational programs, better vocational programs, better living conditions, better food, better visits, better contact with our family members, and so many other things that could benefit us. I admit that the Bureau of Prisons allowed inmates all of those things at one time or another, but 90% of the time, it is us that self-destruct, ruin it for ourselves, and the Central Office in Washington, D.C. end up taking all of these benefits away from us. It's not that they want to, but our primitive barbarian ways, and attitudes, force them to do the things they do to us. Examples, at one time we controlled the running of Lewisburg, Leavenworth, and Atlanta, and all we did was murder, kill, rape, assault and disrespect each other every chance we got. All we did was preach hate against each other, go to war against each other in groups and gangs, and destroy what had been given to us. Brutality is usually a must in these prisons with each other, cynicism, tragedy, and absurdity go hand in hand in these places. We have no noble purpose in these places, other than the Jail House Law Clerks, or the Jail House Lawyers trying to win their "FREEDOM" by doing law work, day and night, studying and researching, trying desperately and diligently for a hearing or a win in the courts. Those guys are the Real Comrades. Prison is a synonym for destruction, death, pain and constant drama. Ordinarily men, cannot make it in these types or places. WHY? Because in order to survive and live in these types of environments you cannot maintain yourself on an ordinary level as a human being, not after going through the things you experience in these places. You do have guys that come out of these places, though, who redeem themselves by education, or doing the things they like doing and achieve unimaginable greatness, such Malcom X, Eigih Mohammad Nelson Mandela, Robert Magmbe, and many others.

Some of these guys have great influence and power over other inmates in these prisons. They are called shot callers, but most of the shot callers, plain and simple, are unintelligent and send their inmate soldiers to do very stupid things. Most of the shot callers are not respected for how intelligent they are, but for how physical they can be. Usually 90% of the time, an inmate is not respected for how intelligent he is in these prisons, but for how physically dangerous he is. All we do is hurt each other. Try to understand me, as you read into the depth of my mind while you read this book. Some of these guys are actually, legally, and factually innocent of the crime they were sentenced to, and that's real. However, that means nothing to these guys. Why? Because they are in here with you and you have to do what you have to in order to survive, even if it means an innocent man, protecting himself in order to stay alive or surviving in these places under any circumstances necessary. Even if that circumstance ends up being murder, assault, or killing another inmate in order to stop him from killing or murdering you. Prison is a violent place to live and exist in.

Some of the things I say in this book, other inmates may not like, but so what, I've been here for 23 years of my life and it is not like what I'm saying is not true.

Life in prison is exactly that life without the possibility of parole. You never go home, you are isolated from society for the rest of your natural life in a controlled conditional sub-human society. If they (Bureau of Prisons) can control your condition, then they can control your environment. In prison the Bureau of Prisons controls both. It's a damn shame how over 217 thousand inmates in the Federal Bureau of Prisons, cannot come together and stick together for a decent cause. We would rather kill and murder each other, than to stand together for parole, for better living conditions, for better law libraries, for better education. But once they (Bureau of Prisons) give it to us, we (inmates) will turn right around and give it all back to them, based on our disrespect for each other, and the things we do to each other, and then we blame it on the system all over again. We as inmates, don't even try to pull together completely throughout the system for a decent cause. We hate each other, we are racist toward each other, all we do is talk about each other, belittle one another. Every now and then we might have something positive to say about each other, but most of the time it's negativity toward one another. We hang in groups most of us in these prisons, which is usually by states, and or with gangs from all over the world, not just all over the country, but all over the world in these prisons.

It's basically the same thing in these prisons every single day, recreation, vocational, and educational programs that the inmates usually don't or simply for some stupid reason or another won't or refuse to take advantage of positively. The law library is never filled to its capacity, which should be over filled every day that it is open. Inmates stay as far away from the law library as they can. Rather than go home or try to find a constitutional, or statute errors in their case or prove their innocence, they (inmates) would rather play basketball all day, every day, and sit around and be lazy and do simply nothing but waste away in these places. Only a very few inmates try to educate themselves, or better themselves in these prisons, most of us want to get back out so we can put down another score, or commit another crime, because that's all we talk about in these prisons is crime, all we do is commit more and more crimes against each other every day, by the things we do to each other every day. We simply have no respect for each other as we should have. Believe me, I live in a mad house constantly surrounded by the most dangerous criminals in the world, not just in the nation, but in the world. Some of them are highly educated, some are highly sophisticated, some are very clever, and shrewd, and influential, but most of them are lames, suckers, chumps, and petty thieves, and were never about anything from the very start. I live in an environment in which one inmate will kill another one over a telephone. I live in an environment where one inmate will murder another inmate because he said he did not like how the other inmate looked at him. I live in a world where if they don't say excuse me for interrupting in another inmate's conversation, he will stab you or stab you to death, and think nothing of it. I live in an environment where inmates will testify and be a witness against each other, where they will testify or set up a correctional officer that tried to help them, or was trying to help them, and the other inmates use some twisted logic in why he set this officer up and got the officer sent to jail for helping him eat, helping him survive, helping him live better. This is where I've been living now for 23 years of my life, and it will be forever where I live if I don't win my case in court because I'm serving 4 life terms plus a ball ten, 110 years, without release and only by death. It's madness, it's confusing at times, it's unhealthy mentally most of the time, but I've been here so long, I've honestly become immune to it now, I no longer feel it, I now usually see it before it comes my way, whatever it is. There is no pain, no hurt, and no sorrow. That's for the weak in these places, you must always be strong and focused in these places or you will definitely cease to exist. It's how you live in these places.

In the Prison Mess Hall, there's usually about 15 correctional officers or more in and outside, the Warden, Assistant Warden, Program Warden, Records Officers, who can tell you about your record or if you have other charges pending against you, there is the Captain, Lt's, Case Managers, Counselors, Nurses, School Teachers, and School Supervisors. If there's any questions you want to ask, you can go up to these individuals and ask those questions. The Mess Hall is a very dangerous place, because at any time, a fight, stabbing, or anything can happen, and cause a riot, or a hostage situation, or someone gets hurt badly because there are so many peoples, at least 500 inmates are in there during lunch, and dinner, depending on what kind of meal they are having. So you have to be on your best behavior in the Mess Hall, plus, never jump in front of an inmate or skip the lines; that can cause a problem, such as get you stabbed to death, because the guy might say you disrespected him by jumping in front of him in the line, or that you never asked him to go in front of him. Usually if you are in a federal penitentiary, a physical problem with result from this violation, but if you are in a medium security prison, you'll usually get a verbal reprimand from the other inmates.

Inmates steal everything out of the Mess Hall, no matter what it is, they'll steal it and sell it to each other. They'll even kill each other or stab each other over certain things in the Mess Hall, such as if they hide some foodstuffs that they have stolen, and you steal it from them, they'll stab you, or kill you, or verbally check you for stealing from them, if they find out it's you that stole it. When you enter the Mess Hall, in all penitentiaries it's usually a metal detector that searches you before you enter it, to make sure you are not carrying any weapons or steel. Then you are sometimes checked when you leave out by a correctional officer, in some mediums they use the same process and then in other medium facilities, they don't have any metal detectors at all. It depends on what medium you are in. The food is usually not that bad, but it's been changing and getting worse over the years that I've been incarcerated. It's to the point now that if the Bureau of Prisons feeds you reasonably like a human being, the correctional officers will picket and protest against the prison, and try and fabricate and say the inmates are eating better than citizens on the streets. There's absolutely no truth to that, but the correctional union will still protest against the prison, and walk around outside with prison signs saying that inmates eat better than them. No matter what an inmate is in prison for, 99% of the correctional officers and staff are going to hate your guts, dislike you, talk bad to you, disrespect you, beat you, cripple you physically, and even kill you, and 99% of the time get away with it. Because they have the best lawyers, the best of everything at their disposal to help them. Now you have some good counselors, and some good case managers and a few good wardens that don't look at you like that and will respect you as a human being, such as Warden Holt, and his brother Ronnie Holt, Mr. Wanger that was in Lewisburg, a case manager, Mr. Painter that was in Schuylkill, Pennsylvania, who was a case manager, Mr. Wanger who was in Atlanta a case manager, Mr. Bout-it-Bout-it, who was at Atlanta a correctional officer. These people did their jobs and then there was Mr. Gage, a case manager at Coleman F.C.I. Medium, in Florida, and Mr. Davis, and Mr. Degarate, Mr. Martin, Mr. Garland, and Ms. Smalls, they were all very great people and they would honestly help you if they could. But then there are those that hate your guts because you are a prisoner, and will not help you at all and dare you to say something about it, so they can get you locked up for 23 hours a day, or every chance they get.

Some of them you can see the hate in them. The Bureau of Prisons tell them when they train them to don't believe nothing an inmate says to you, don't trust them, stare them down, keep them in fear, let them know you control the units or unit you are working in if one is at the door trying to get in, make him wait until he is good and ready to let him in the door, don't talk to none of them, unless they ask you a question, keep them away from you period. If you have any problem out of any of them press this button that you have on your side and we will be right there, we will do whatever is necessary even if it means justifying a murder on them, or him. The correctional officers will talk to you so rudely that if you have no control you'll be in prison for the rest of your life, 23 hours a day in a cell, or dead. They'll strap you on a 4 point bed and leave you there for hours at a time, while you urinate on yourself or defecate on yourself or if you have medical problems, dead on that journey. They will murder, assault or attack you in front of 200 or 300 inmates, and 99% of the time, not one of those inmates will step a foot up to help and/or assist you from getting beat to death, or assaulted or murdered. Why? Because those inmates are afraid of the system, of correctional officers' uniforms alone, they are afraid what the uniform represents, and what power it holds. The inmates would rather kill each other than protect each other, when it comes to that uniform. They (inmates) will do everything in their power to avoid helping each other when it comes to that uniform. All these groups and gangs in these prisons, all they do is self-destruct, all they do is assault and kill each other, all they do is harm each other and call each other racist names. I live in a world where inmates in Federal prisons are afraid to stand up for positive things such as a better education, better food, better living conditions, better programs. They would rather assault and kill each other before they do anything positive like that. I live in a world where my fellow inmates love being out of their cells, but won't lock down voluntarily for better living conditions, parole, better treatment, better medical treatment because they let us die all the time without any real medical attention, take an aspirin, there's nothing wrong with you inmate, and then suddenly you are dead, and the other inmates won't say a damn thing in your defense to help and assist you. But they'll go right out in that yard and kill each other over a baseball game, or basketball game or because they don't like each other. We are self-destructive in these Federal prisons, all we do is hurt and kill each other. All we do is negativity, not all of us, but 99% of us do, and then that's giving too much, it's more like 99.5%.

In these prisons any of them in the United States, inmates, will kill, murder, stab, rape, assault each other, all the time, but they won't ask for a better law library that will help and assist them in getting their "FREEDOM" they won't ask for better programs like in education, and vocation, so they can prepare themselves for society upon release. They don't ask for better food, especially the way they feed us in some of these prisons. They don't ask for better medical care, or for positive things that will help and benefit them. All these guys want to do is watch sports, play sports, kill each other, argue with others, assault each other, rape and kill each other and verbally disrespect each other. They don't run these Federal prisons, the correctional officers and prison Administration run them. It's a damn shame, how they have at least 50 different types of gangs or more in these Federal prisons, and all they do is hate against each other, stab and kill each other, because they are racist against each other, but they won't band together for a common cause like parole, better educational and vocational programs to save their own lives. These are the same guys that a lot of you think was the real deal, you looked up to them, you highly respected them, well, a lot of them if you could just see how they conduct themselves in these prisons you would lose all of that respect you have or had for them.

You know how your friends or someone tells you just mind your business while you are in prison, and you'll be just fine, well it's easy for someone to tell you that who has never been incarcerated, because the ones minding their business, and trying to stay clear of problems, they are having problems and serious problems. Why? Because there are guys in these prisons looking for problems, some of them are never going home or will ever be released, a lot of them don't work on their cases, trying to find fundamental errors or trying to prove their innocence, they've given up, some completely, so they look for someone who's minding their own business, one who's trying to work on his case, or doing something positive for himself, and they create an unnecessary conflict with the guy trying to stay away from unnecessary conflicts. It happens all the time, and then a body jumps off, assault takes place, something serious and crucial goes down, it's a major beef, it's a major lock down. Why? Because that guy who was minding his own business had to physically punish the guy looking for problems unnecessarily. These are some vicious places, and you must immediately learn how to handle yourself if you intend on surviving in them so you can make it out alive or intact. It's important you work out physically in these places, all the time you have to stay prepared for anything that may happen, or you try to prevent yourself from getting sick, because the administration doesn't like sending you to the hospital, because you are an inmate and a security risk at that. So working out is usually a must, especially if you are in a Federal penitentiary.

If I were you, I would never commit a crime. I'd suggest you get a nice education or a job, or do something constructive other than committing crimes for a living. And if you must commit a crime let it be a non-violent crime, because you'll be able to at least be free one day. Crimes like child molestation, child crimes, hurting the elderly, hurting little children, or hurting an innocent family, or rape, or an unnecessary crime, you better not come to prison, because you are going to have problems if the other inmates find out about you, especially crimes like that. Homosexuality happens in prisons, some guys get raped, some volunteer and become homosexuals on their own, but inmates do not go around just raping each other. That's simply not true. Men have sex with each other in these Federal prisons, but it is not on a mass scale, as the Bureau of Prisons would have you to believe. I repeat clearly to you, homosexuality is not a major problem in any of the prisons. I've been in eight of them and four of those, very high security, and homosexuality was not a major problem, but it is going on, and it will always go on in prisons. Some guys act like women, and some want to be a woman, but the mass majority of inmates are not into any homosexuality at all. It's a myth to think otherwise. I know because I'm here and I've been in here for over 23 years of my life. 99% of the guys are not into it at all.

Prison life as a whole is very dangerous, intelligent, unintelligent, retarded, immature, brilliant, crazy gangsters and a lot of other things. One thing you will definitely learn in these prisons is psychology, physical psychology, body language for sure, and mental psychology, it is a must you learn to read your opponent and all those around you immediately, you must learn your surroundings as well, all of that is a must, it helps you stay alive in these places.

There's approximately 1700 different

personalities in this Federal prison, that I am presently stationed at here in Coleman, Florida. I have to deal with all of them every single day. I've been dealing with them for approximately 23 years already. In these places you learn to read body language, feel energy, see physically and read mentally body language very well. You learn to do it and recognize it very fast too, your life depends on it every single day that you are in these places. For example, I can see you and read your body language and feel your energy by looking at you, as to how you are responding or acting and know that something is good, bad, or whatever, I'll know within five minutes at most. If I speak to you, I'll know as soon as I'm finished speaking to you, because I'm reading you physically, mentally and feeling your energy from your body. If I walk in a prison, I can tell you immediately what the prison temperature is in that prison, I can feel if it's a good place to be, a bad or negative, and I can tell you if it's a prison of constant death, murder, stabbings or if it's an in-between or what. I'll know as soon as I step on the compound in that prison. It took years to see and learn how to survive in these prisons. I had no other choice but to learn them, and learn them fast, or I would have never survived in these places as long as I have.

You can never be weak in these places, always stand up no matter what the circumstances might entail. Some inmates don't stand up though, they allow themselves to be raped, disrespected mentally, and physically. Some inmates allow other inmates to apply peer pressure to them and not think for themselves. Some inmates are followers. They'll do anything to be accepted even murder, kill, or assault each other, or whatever you tell him to do. Some inmates are afraid to stand up for themselves, by himself; he needs his crew to stand with him. Some prisoners are just plain robots, dam fools, lames, chumps, and suckers, and some are very manipulative, influential and persuasive. Some inmates, you just can't communicate with, because some of them are very mentally unstable, there's always a crew of them hanging together too, and they'll murder you, stab you or assault you, and get away with it, because they are classified as mentally deranged.

You have correctional officers, counselors, case managers, Captains, Lt's, Assistant Wardens, and Wardens in those Federal prisons, some of them just are here to make sure you do your time while incarcerated, and that is it. But you have others among them, all they do is cause inmates problems, intentionally, and deliberately for absolutely no apparent reason at all. Because they simply don't like inmates at all. Even though they are not here for them to like you or not. Some of them take it personally among themselves, to hate you, despise you, hurt you, kill you, assault you, and strip you of all of your God given rights by any means necessary. To some of them you are nothing but a slave, to them you are worse than a slave, you are whatever they want you to be to some of them, and to 90% of inmates that won't stand up to those types of Federal officials.

At the Correctional Officers Training School, they teach them to hate you, never to believe nothing you say, they tell their officers never go against another officer for an inmate.

CHAPTER THIRTY-FIVE

PRISONERS, PLEASE REMEMBER THAT:

"The credit belongs to the man who is actually in the arena, whose face is marred by dust, sweat, and blood, who strives valiantly, who errs and comes up short, again, and again, because there is no effort without error of shortcoming, but who knows the great enthusiast, the great devotionist, who spends himself for a worthy cause; who at best, knows in the end the triumph of high achievement, and who, at the worst if he fails, at least he fails while daring greatly, so that his place shall never be with those cold and timid souls who knew neither victory or defeat". "NO MATTER WHAT"!

If left as is, we still continue as we are: "slaves," in a very dangerous prison system, constantly subjected to a horrific environment and persistent sub-human conditions, constantly failing at everything we do because we do not try to stand up, so we have no alternative, but to lose in constant failure, because we are not standing up for anything. So please my fellow prisoners, will you stand with the rest of us for a better and more positive future? You must remember and always keep in mind, that some of us may be, even many of us, will face adverse prejudice from each other, and even hardship, but we must at least try to stand as one against this very cruel and un just system, or we will continue to lack better medical care, better living conditions and programs. My fellow prisoners, please, we live in a world where we have no love and respect for each other, where we must stop what we are doing to one another, and band together in unity, no matter what the situation and circumstances turn out to be.   If we should fail in our attempts for a better prison future, that any prisoner should want to stand up for, then at least we failed while daring sincerely to make a better and more constructive life for ourselves. We did not lay down like the timid and the weak who know of neither success nor defeat in their struggle because they continue to do nothing at all, but what they continue to do all day to day, and then submit to an unjust, prejudiced prison system, against all minorities, and whoever else that is confined in these prisons with us, being treated exactly as we are every single day like slaves and animals constantly at the mercy of a terrible and dreadful system, that has absolutely no respect at all for those of the timid and weak, nor for the brave and strong either. I've wanted to go to the mess hall many a times and stand on the table before all of my fellow prisoners and scream out to them "My brothers will you stand up with me in this struggle for a better prison future for us all? Will you please from this day on help me help US all stand together, and whatever the circumstances turn out to be, at least we stood together as one for a great cause, and whether we succeed or fail, at least we will know that we tried to help ourselves."

At least we will know that we did not decease in vain without just cause for the struggle of a better future. At least we will know that there will be others that follow and pursue our struggle for the very purpose that we might not now succeed in accomplishing. And at least we refused to stop allowing ourselves to be degraded, disrespected and treated like slaves and animals under such abnormal and sub-human conditions, which we are subjected to in these places every single day. We simply have nothing to lose, but a lot to gain if we would just communicate and get ourselves together.

CHAPTER THIRTY-SIX

MY FELLOW PRISONERS-PLEASE

My fellow prisoners, please, give me, yourself, and others the opportunity to stand up strong, non-violently for what we all believe in, which is FREEDOM, respect, and better opportunities for the future upon our release from these places. We are already at our lowest level. We can't get any worse than we already are, telling on each other, killing each other, stabbing and assaulting each other, raping each other, turning each other into mental patients and degrading each other every single day in these places with negativity.

I need you all to just think about what we are doing to ourselves in these places. How we are treating each other. My fellow prisoners, we are at the point of no return, if we don't change our way of living in these places. We need to stand with each other for positive change. We receive extremely too much time in these places. The Laws are geared to keep us extremely too long incarcerated in these prisons. We must start right here in these prisons for change, what better place to start from than in these Federal prisons. America, the greatest country in the world with the largest prison system in the world with the longest prison sentences in the world. Life, multi-life, triple life, 10, 20 30, years for little or no drugs at all. Made up organizations by the FEDS, just to give us longer sentences, so much time to serve, that the world changes on us, several times before we know it. Too much time, too long of a time. Most of it is strictly based on the color of our skin. Will you all just please, just stop for a second and look at what's going on with us in these places. I often flash back to the stories and books I was told and read about in George Jackson in prison letters, in ROAD TO HELL, I think about James Carr in the book "BAD". I think about Tookie Williams and his book. I think about Gary Gilmore, Jack Henry Abbot, and many other books that were about these prisons and how these prisoners struggled, and what they experienced. And of course, I did not forget you Willie Bostic, your book was well understood. I need all Federal prisoners to read this book, and understand what I am saying, not try to understand, but to clearly understand me and my way of saying what I am saying. Am I asking you to rise up? YES!! I am, but in a non-violent way, without violence. I need you to look at what we are up against, what we will continue to face if we do not stand up for ourselves and for those who are coming behind us. I need you to stand up for yourself, so that you too, will have a better future. This is the right time, the right place, and the right way to show not only America, but the world, that we too, are human beings, not the criminals, indentured servants, and slaves that we have been depicted as being. We are not scum, garbage, or trash, and we refuse to be treated as such, especially in the greatest country that the world has ever known.

The President says all the time that we Americans live in the greatest country in the Free World. And now the world's greatest prisoners demand positive and constructive change in a Federal system riddled with hatred, murder, assault, rape, ignorance, stupidly retardation, brutality, and YES! Suicide on a constant basis. I need you to help me help you all to change our degenerate way of life in these places to a much better way of living in these places. But we will only succeed if we all stand together as one, non-violently. We cannot win any other way. But, this way we can change Federal prison history, and this we must do, or we will forever be treated as we are being treated right now, which is terrible.

I say to you, all my fellow prisoners, some of us might not make it through the struggle for a better future, but we must try any way. Some of us will complain and cry about nothing, some of us will use all kinds of rhetoric and verbal tools not to stand up, but we must, we have to, or many of us will decease here, become old here, get sick here, and many others so we must at least try and try hard to bring to the world, not only to America, but to the world what we are going through, and how we are being treated in these prisons in America. I need you all to stand with me, and be with me to the very end. For those of you who refuse, and won't stand for something, you will always be as they say, "You are nothing!" Because you won't stand up even for your own FREEDOM, even for a better future, and even for the betterment of your fellow prisoners who need you to stand strong and firm with them to the very end.

CHAPTER THIRTY-SEVEN

FLASHBACK - 2014

I flashed back into the system and how we as prisoners are powerless amongst ourselves. We know that the power is within us and by us to stand up for what we believe in, which is for a better system, and a better way of being respected. Our distress and failure amongst each other pains me because we keep choosing to fail, rather than succeed in a struggle that will either break us or push us to prison history for the better, especially for those who will come behind us. Our stubbornness, incompetence, ignorance, stupidity, and selfishness against each other will get us nowhere, but pushed back even further than we already are.

It pains me to know that my Attica, New York brothers, my Lucasville, Ohio brothers, my George Jackson, California brothers and Louisiana brothers in Angola, all died for nothing. Nothing, in the sense that we refuse to respect their struggle, their plight, their courage to want more for us all legitimately in a system that murders, assaults and kill us with impunity. Nothing is ever done about it, because even the public has been trained by the media to reject what is so sincerely in our hearts and minds for a better rehabilitation of ourselves. If as prisoners, we would just stop the madness against each other, and struggle together subjectively with endurance as one, we would surely achieve our goal of respect, better programs, better medical care, better rehabilitation programs, good time, and parole.

It's nothing that we should not already have, but we refuse to stand up for it. We refuse to sacrifice for it. We refuse to stop the madness against each other. We refuse to come together as one and be proud of each other and help one another in this prison struggle to have a better life than the horrific one which we are presently living. All I ask is for you to try to help yourself. Try to stand with me. I can't do it all by myself. If I could, I would, but I need you all to stand with me. If you can watch t.v. all day every day, then you can stand with me for something worth standing for. If you can play tickets, play cards, and sports all day, then you can stand with me. If you can assault, murder, and kill each other as we always do, then you can stand with me for as long as it takes to get respect, better programs, a better future, better medical care, reasonable good time, parole, and a change in the Laws for these drug crimes, for us all. If you can do all of these self-destructive things against each other and get locked down for months, and years, at a time for negativity and stupidity, then my brothers, you can stand with me in this prison struggle, gaining positivity for us all. I need your might, your strength, and your endurance if I can myself attempt to succeed, because I need you with me. Whether you know it or not you are me, and I am you in this prison struggle. Whether you like it or not we are as one and only as one will we endure or we will never be respected. If we do not stand up, we will continue to be treated as animals, slaves, and indentured servants. We will forever suffer in a system intentionally and deliberately geared toward failure, our failure, because we won't stand up for anything worth standing up for. We stay as non-persons, and that is how the American public and the world see us. But my fellow prisoners, we can change that by standing together as one, and by not stopping until we accomplish what we set out to accomplish and achieve. Please, my brothers, I need you, and you know we need each other. You also know that it is time for change.   Time for us to stop living as we are in these places. Therefore, a change has to come, and it can only come through us or else there will never be any in this system. The administration will never ever respect our names, our ethics, and principles which we have amongst ourselves. My brothers we have to move forward now, while we are able, while we can, or the fight, the struggle, and our endurance will only get worse than it already is.

My brothers, we live in a world mystified by failure- a world lacking confidence in one another. A world that I'm so tired of after 24 years of assaults, murders, killings, disrespect, negativity, and ignorance towards each other. We need change in this world in which we are living. We must seek it, and we must start now, while there is still hope, and still a way to do so with each other.

One day we will look at each other with respect for the cause that we fought so hard and struggled for, and thank those who helped us in our fight, and in our struggle for a better future.

No matter how long it takes, and what we must endure, we must do this, my brothers, and we must start now, immediately or we will forever be degraded, distressed, disrespected, and treated as animals, slaves, and indentured servants in a slave plantation system, that is strictly geared toward doing what it does to us which is to totally disrespect us in any way they (administration) see fit to do so. My brothers, we have to stop this and move forward to a better future in these places, or else we will surely suffer a mental, spiritual and educational death. We must, therefore, be determined to fight and struggle for a better future in these sub-human conditions, which we stay constantly subjected to every day. We have no malice nor hatred for the Federal Bureau of Prisons as they so viciously do against us in their training, and line ups, and monthly training case managers reviews of us. All we want is respect and to be treated as human beings, with better programs to educate ourselves, better medical so that we stop dying so rapidly in these places, better law libraries, reasonable good time, and parole. That is all we are asking for. Even though we anticipate that the Federal Bureau of Prisons will not respect our wishes and grievances, which are minor and very reasonable. We will fight and stand, and endure with all of our might until we achieve and accomplish victory in our struggle for a better future in the in Federal Bureau of Prisons.

CHAPTER THIRTY-EIGHT

SLY GREEN
TWENTY-THREE YEARS LATER

I must admit that I am grateful and now humbled by the fact that I had to stand strong and firm, in order to get to where I am now. I am aware of the circumstances and conditions that I unknowingly subjected myself to throughout my 23 plus years of incarceration in Federal and New York State prisons. I am mindful of the sacrifices I had to make with the birth of my two young sons, and my daughter, to have to be away from them, for so many years in order to do what I had to do, just so my family members would able to continue to live in the City of Buffalo, New York in which I was born and raised.

The challenges I have faced while being incarcerated all of these years have been many, mostly consisting of jealousy, fabrications, misunderstandings, stumbling blocks, and hurdles that I had to get over or around in order to get to where I am now. I have transformed into one of the best jail house pro-se litigants I could possibly be in order to win and succeed in gaining my own "FREEDOM" or else I will never ever be released from Federal custody.

I can never crumble under pressure and or fall into mental ruin, or my life and dream to regain my FREEDOM would surely be over. I simply cannot afford a calamity. I cannot afford a crisis nor to be at war with fools, because the challenge I've been facing for 23 years is real, serious, and detrimental if I do not succeed. I have to meet it and win it, or I'll die as the convict Donald G. Green, #39747-019, in a Federal United

States Penitentiary never ever seeing FREEDOM again.

I do apologize for my way of life, and I have wavered far away from it, because of the consequences of it, which I never ever want to experience again.

23 years ago, I was looked at as a Crime Boss, a Leader, a gangster, a Drug Lord, a Drug King Pin, a notorious Drug Boss, running a vicious criminal organization, or gang or crew or Enterprise. Those are the things that were said about me in newspaper articles, books, and magazines. But, now, I'm strictly into being the best jail house pro-se litigant I can be in order to win my FREEDOM. With a case so fabricated as mine, no lawyer is going to get me my FREEDOM. I have to do it myself or die trying. I no longer believe everything they say to me. I highly respect lawyers, and would have loved to have been one, especially after learning what I've learned thus far. I would love nothing more than to work for and with lawyers and win cases. All I want to do is win cases. I love law, and I love America too. I have nothing against my country. I simply don't blame anyone for anything. I'm here because of "me" and yes, I do have a much longer sentence, than Gotti, and the Uni bomber put together. That's no question, it is because I am African American and I do say that there was prejudice in my sentencing. Otherwise, I have no complaints and I just have to win or die trying, because I'm never giving up. I'm going to fight until I win or until I can't fight any more, which would be because I am dead and gone.

I'm just not the type of guy that blames anybody for my own misgivings or problems. If I win, I win, if I never do, then it'll never be because I didn't put all I had into winning. I've read all kinds of books on law, on Judges, on Lawyers, on U.S. Attorneys and any and everything to do with law. Believe me, if I don't get free, it won't ever be because I gave up. Pro-se jail house litigants don't give up. Walker, Meeka, Mr. Skinner, Rusty, Tommy Rutledge, Tampa Mase, St. Louis Leon, As-Sadiq, Young Magnum, and many others helped me become who I am now, because I could never have done it alone without them.

I live in World where I'm hardly in prison, it's called the pro-se litigant world, and it's a world of constant legal battles, and scrambles and sometimes BIG WARS with giant issues that take our whole Firm to win.

I live in a world that's never ending, that's always changing, and therefore, it keeps me positive and on a constructive path, a legal path, a path channeled only toward the only direction I've ever wanted to travel for the last 23 years of my life. That's to a destination called FREEDOM. I must admit, it's been hard and difficult many times, but, I have 4 life terms, plus a ball 10, so whether difficult or not I've got to keep going until I get there- if I get there or whenever I get there. It's the only direction of travel that makes any legal, logical, or rational sense to me. As we all know under my circumstances and the sub-human conditions that I am constantly being faced with, losing is not an option so no matter how many times I fall in the courts, I know that I must find a new and different Federal Statute, or Section 3582 (c)(2) motion, or 60(B) motion, or Section 2241(c)(3) motion, or Great Writ, or whatever it takes to win my FREEDOM. I cannot give up because if I do, that is the day I die a convict. That's why I stay engrossed in law. Time simply does not exist to me when I'm into law. Days turn into weeks, weeks, turn into months, and months turn into years without me ever noticing it. I hardly give a thought to the outside world.

No one in the world exists when I'm into my law books, or on the computer. All I'm thinking is FREEDOM, or winning a case. This is my world. I lose myself in it completely and sometimes as I've just stated, I don't come back for weeks, months, or years. Then, sometimes, I don't want to come back, but I have to because the research of the case, or the case must be finalized for print to the courts. Then suddenly I come back into a world unbeknownst to those who have no idea of what goes on in it, but for the exception of those that live in the world from which I must endure until I gain my FREEDOM.

I came from a world of FREEDOM 23 years ago. The state of New York murder conviction put me away for 25 years to life, by trial. 18 months later, a Federal Grand Jury toppled me and crushed me with 4 life terms plus 110 years in a Federal United States Penitentiary for the rest of my natural life. Shackles, chains, handcuffs, a military helicopter and the strictest security in the city's history took me down forever- if I were to accept it as such. I can't just sit here for the rest of my natural life watching t.v., going to recreation, looking at movies, talking on the phone, stabbing and killing other convicts, or gossiping about this or that, or living in these conditions. They have lawyers, doctors, a billionaire, many millionaires, Drug Lords, King Pins, killers, murders, con men, hustlers, pimps, you name it, they are here. But I'm simply not trying to spend the rest of my life in here with them. I have to fight for mine, and believe me, God only helps those who help themselves, especially in a situation such as my own. I see things in life so much different now, my views and opinions have changed about a lot of things, especially how I used to think. Being incarcerated should make anyone want to change. Especially with a person serving life plus 25, and 4 life terms plus a Ball 10, in Federal and State prisons with no possibility of ever being released except through a miracle or by winning his case in court. I've changed, mentally, spiritually, and educationally. I'm no longer the guy I once was and the way I was portrayed and depicted by the media. I never was that guy anyway. But I know as I walk this legal path to someday regain my FREEDOM, that I cannot and I must not ever falter, or cause myself any unnecessary legal mishaps, unnecessarily in the courts, because If I do without proper and legitimate reason, I'll never ever see the light of day ever again.   I must stay relevant in the law, and my ideals and thoughts all geared to one day being a "FREE MAN," it's all I have to live for! FREEDOM! FREEDOM!!

CHAPTER THIRTY-NINE

ENDING

Still after all these years, and even on triple O.G. status, at times I need all of my strength to deal with the constant madness around me, which I have unfortunately exposed myself to unnecessarily. So with all of the doubts, trials, tribulations, and yes, uncertainties, I had no idea that my life would turn out like this. I can't complain now, because I'm not a complainer. I just have to do the best I can with the hand I've dealt myself. And so I continue to pray, hope, and constantly stay trying to win my "FREEDOM" for that is really the only thing I live for in this place. If I really felt in my heart and soul, that I was never ever going to win my "FREEDOM," I would have ceased to exist a long time ago, or I would be locked down 23-7 in ADX, at Florence, Colorado. BUT, I have a plan and that is a plan for "FREEDOM," my "FREEDOM!"

Even though I now have the knowledge to free myself, at one time I had nothing but hope and guesswork and a lot of imagination. Now I see the light. I feel the sun, and every so often I might get a rainy day every now and then, but I know now that everything I've learned in that law library for the last 23 years I needed in order to endure and fight the legal challenges and battles that are constantly in my paperwork, trying to prevent me from gaining access to my freedom. I am doing the very best I can with what I have to win my freedom, and I say to those of you who wish and want to follow or travel this journey that I once did — my advice to you is DON'T! It is a journey unlike many, it is a destructive and very negative way of life. It's a world too complicated for the average human being. It's a journey simply not worth traveling at all. You should know that from reading this book. For those of you who are foolish enough to even attempt the journey which I traveled is crazy, and totally insane. So I say to you, please do not try it for your own sake!

Made in the USA
Las Vegas, NV
16 April 2024